THE STUDENT LEADERSHIP CHALLENGE

Facilitation and Activity Guide

JB JOSSEY-BASS™

A Wiley Brand

THE STUDENT LEADERSHIP CHALLENGE

Facilitation and Activity Guide

James Kouzes and Barry Posner

With Beth High and Gary M. Morgan

WILEY

Cover image: Shutterstock
Cover design: Adrian Morgan
Copyright © 2013 by John Wiley & Sons, Inc. All rights reserved.

Published by Jossey-Bass
A Wiley Imprint
One Montgomery Street, Suite 1200, San Francisco, CA 94104-4594—www.josseybass.com

Jossey-Bass books and products are available through most bookstores. To contact Jossey-Bass directly call our Customer Care Department within the U.S. at 800-956-7739, outside the U.S. at 317-572-3986, or fax 317-572-4002.

Wiley publishes in a variety of print and electronic formats and by print-on-demand. Some material included with standard print versions of this book may not be included in e-books or in print-on-demand. If this book refers to media such as a CD or DVD that is not included in the version you purchased, you may download this material at http://booksupport.wiley.com. For more information about Wiley products, visit www.wiley.com.

ISBN: 978-1-118-39008-5 (paper)
ISBN: 978-1-118-60256-0 (ebk.)
ISBN: 978-1-118-60257-7 (ebk.)
ISBN: 978-1-118-60258-4 (ebk.)

Printed in the United States of America
FIRST EDITION

PB Printing   SKY10028197_071521

CONTENTS

Module 3: Model the Way: Practice Overview and Guided Discussion

Module 4: Inspire a Shared Vision: Practice Overview and Guided Discussion

Module 5: Challenge the Process: Practice Overview and Guided Discussion

THE STUDENT LEADERSHIP CHALLENGE

Facilitation and Activity Guide

Welcome to The Student Leadership Challenge

There is no shortage of challenges that require exemplary leadership. Leaders help others meet these challenges. Student leaders will help those they influence face the immediate issues of today and eventually lead the long-term development of people, communities, and institutions so they can adapt, change, prosper, and grow. The core philosophy of *The Student Leadership Challenge*® disputes the myth that leadership is something that you find only at the top of the class or as the person running a student organization. Leadership is not about position or title, power or authority, celebrity or wealth, family or genetics. It's also not just something for a chosen few. Rather, leadership is everyone's business.

Moreover, leadership is an identifiable set of skills and abilities that is available to everyone. It is about relationships, personal credibility, and what leaders do. It's about an observable set of skills and abilities that are useful wherever a leader may be. Given the motivation and desire, leadership is a skill that can be strengthened, honed, and enhanced through practice and feedback, following role models, and coaching. If students find themselves in a challenging situation that requires setting a good example for others, looking ahead to the future, taking initiative to change the status quo, building teamwork and trust, and encouraging others to succeed, they are in a situation that requires leadership. What is required of them in this situation is that they step forward and become the best leader they can be.

The Student Leadership Challenge is about how students mobilize others to want to make extraordinary things happen in their schools, communities, and organizations. It's an evidence-based framework that describes the practices student leaders use to transform values into actions, visions into realities, obstacles into innovations, separateness into solidarity, and risks into rewards. It shows how students can create the climate in which people turn challenging opportunities into remarkable successes.

It's been said that the education and development of people is the lever to change the world, and we believe this is especially true for young people. In these extraordinary times, the challenges seem only to be increasing in number and complexity. But remember that all generations confront their own serious threats and receive their own favorable circumstances. The abundance of challenges is not the issue: it's how our young people respond to them that matters. Through their responses, they have the potential to seriously worsen or profoundly improve the world in which we live.

Yours is a noble cause. By improving a student's ability to lead, you will directly affect the kinds of positive changes that our world needs. You will make a difference in the quality of the life of your students and those they will influence throughout their lives. We know from our research that every student has the capacity to learn to lead and the capacity to make extraordinary things happen. We believe in them, we believe in you, and we thank you for challenging yourself to liberate and develop the leader in every student.

ABOUT *THE STUDENT LEADERSHIP CHALLENGE*

The foundation of the approach set out in this book is The Five Practices of Exemplary Leadership® model. The model began as a research project in 1983 that asked people, "What did you do when you were at your 'personal best' in leading others?"

Three decades later, the model continues to prove its effectiveness as a clear, evidence-based path to achieving the extraordinary—for individuals, teams, organizations, and communities. It turns the abstract concept of leadership into easy-to-grasp practices and behaviors that can be taught; anyone who is willing to step up and accept the challenge to lead can learn them. The model is supported by a core philosophy arising from ongoing research and is founded on these beliefs:

- Leadership is everyone's business.
- Leadership is learned.
- Leadership is a relationship.
- Leadership development is self-development.
- Leadership is an ongoing process.
- Leadership requires deliberate practice.
- Leadership is an aspiration and a choice.
- Leadership makes a difference.

We highly recommend you have your students read *The Student Leadership Challenge* book to deepen their understanding of The Five Practices by learning about other students who demonstrate the leadership behaviors embedded in the model. The book offers evidence from our research and that of others to support our core philosophy that leadership is everyone's business. It provides case examples of young people who demonstrate each practice and prescribes specific recommendations on what people can do to make each practice their own and to continue their development as a leader. We have pulled quotations from some of these stories from students around the world and sprinkled them throughout *The Student Leadership Challenge Facilitation and Activity Guide* and *Student Workbook and Personal Leadership Journal*. People learn from stories, and the stories and quotations we have included are intended to be both inspiring and encouraging.

THE FIVE PRACTICES OF EXEMPLARY LEADERSHIP

The Five Practices of Exemplary Leadership resulted from an intensive research project to determine the leadership behaviors that are essential to making extraordinary things happen in organizations. This effort has continued over three decades, and the findings have been consistent over time. Despite differences in the context of young people's individual stories, their personal-best leadership experiences have revealed similar patterns of leadership behavior.

The research found that when young leaders are at their personal best, they:

1. *Model the Way:* Clarify values and set the example
   Leaders clarify values by finding their voice and affirming shared values, and they set the example by aligning actions with shared values.
2. *Inspire a Shared Vision:* Envision the future and enlist others
   Leaders envision the future by imagining exciting and ennobling possibilities, and they enlist others in a common vision by appealing to shared aspirations.
3. *Challenge the Process:* Search for opportunities and experiment and take risks
   Leaders search for opportunities by seizing the initiative and looking outward for innovative ways to improve. They experiment and take risks by constantly generating small wins and learning from experience.
4. *Enable Others to Act*: Foster collaboration and strengthen others
   Leaders foster collaboration by building trust and facilitating relationships. They strengthen others by enhancing self-determination and developing competence.
5. *Encourage the Heart*: Recognize contributions and celebrate the values and victories
   Leaders recognize contributions by showing appreciation for individual excellence. They celebrate values and victories by creating a spirit of community.

Over multiple settings and across continents, these Five Practices have survived the test of time. The context has changed since this research project was launched, but the content has remained constant.

HOW TO USE THE *FACILITATION AND ACTIVITY GUIDE*

Instructors and facilitators interact with students in many different ways. You may be leading a workshop in which you have only brief contact with a student or you may be in an ongoing coaching relationship in which you work with a student over time. Regardless of your specific circumstance this *Facilitation and Activity Guide* is intended to support the important role you play in supporting students' development as leaders. We designed it to go beyond the instruction of The Five Practices of Exemplary Leadership model to provide tools for the important work you do: the encouragement and support of students' ongoing journey as developing leaders.

Our position is that all five of the leadership practices should be covered, and they should be covered in the order in which we discuss them in this guide. How you execute this is up to you. We have created a number of possible avenues for you to explore and customize. The *Facilitation and Activity Guide* has been written to provide maximum flexibility, allowing you to teach The Five Practices in a way that accommodates the relationship and time you may have with your students and the setting you are in.

You will notice that throughout this guide we use the term *group*. By *group* we mean any collective organization a student is a member of or is leading: an athletic team, a club or common-interest group, any specialized activity or project, an academic team, or even a class group. We also use the word *leaders* to refer to students we have studied, not just students in formal leadership positions but students just like the ones you are working with who have taken the challenge and worked with others to make extraordinary things happen in groups to which they belong. One of our fundamental beliefs is that leadership is an ongoing process that requires deliberate practice. The *Facilitation and Activity Guide* is structured to help your students succeed in their ongoing developmental journey.

This guide contains nine modules. We begin with an introduction, Module 1, that examines the foundation of *The Student Leadership Challenge*. We describe the personal-best leadership experience activity to establish a personal reference point for students as they explore The Five Practices, and then introduce The Five Practices of Exemplary Leadership model. Module 2 provides an overview of the Student Leadership Practices Inventory (Student LPI) with ideas on how to use it with student groups as a powerful development tool.

Modules 3 through 7 explore each of The Five Practices in depth. We have designed these modules to describe one leadership practice and explain the two essential action components of that practice that student leaders employ to make extraordinary things happen in organizations. Collectively, we refer to these as The Ten Commitments of Leadership (see Figure I.1).

Each of the practice modules also covers the associated six leadership behaviors from the Student LPI and suggests ways students can take action to demonstrate the behaviors more frequently. The relationship between The Five Practices, the Ten Commitments, and the 30 behaviors is diagramed in Figure I.2.

Each practice module contains:

- A practice summary and a review of the two commitments to clarify the main ideas supporting the practice.
- Facilitator Cues for framing the discussion of the practice with students to facilitate their understanding of the practice.
- Ideas for helping students understand and explore the leadership behaviors associated with each practice. The goal of *The Student Leadership Challenge* is to move students to take action and make a personal commitment to ongoing practice.

Figure I.1 The Five Practices and Ten Commitments of Exemplary Leadership

Model the Way	1. Clarify values by finding your voice and affirming shared values. 2. Set the example by aligning actions with shared values.
Inspire a Shared Vision	3. Envision the future by imagining exciting and ennobling possibilities. 4. Enlist others in a common vision by appealing to shared aspirations.
Challenge the Process	5. Search for opportunities by seizing the initiative and looking outward for innovative ways to improve. 6. Experiment and take risks by constantly generating small wins and learning from experience.
Enable Others to Act	7. Foster collaboration by building trust and facilitating relationships. 8. Strengthen others by increasing self-determination and developing competence.
Encourage the Heart	9. Recognize contributions by showing appreciation for individual excellence. 10. Celebrate the values and victories by creating a spirit of community.

Source: The Leadership Challenge, 5th edition, by James M. Kouzes and Barry Z. Posner. San Francisco: Jossey-Bass, 2012.

Figure I.2 The Five Practices Model Structure

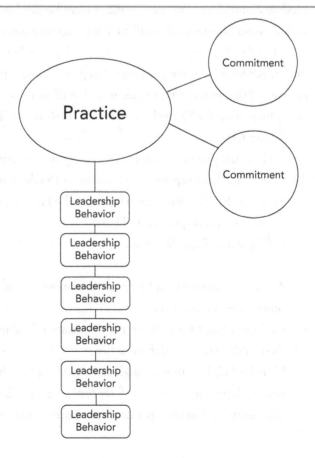

- Sample experiential activities to deepen students' understanding of the practice, including a movie activity to identify stories in film that illustrate The Five Practices and facilitate a deeper understanding of their meaning. These activities are samples for you to use. They are not required and are not an exhaustive list of appropriate exercises. There are many other sources for activities that may work well for the students you are working with. *The Student Leadership Challenge* website offers a treasure trove of resources (www.studentleadershipchallenge.com).
- Ideas for follow-up using the Personal Leadership Journal in Module 8 to enable students to deliberately practice, reflect on, continue learning, and commit to liberating the leader within each of them.

Module 9 contains sample agendas and possible curriculum outlines to get you started in implementing your own development initiative.

We end this guide by quoting the closing to the *Student Workbook*, which is intended to be inspirational for the students participating in a leadership development initiative, and suggest that you provide them similar encouragement, in your own words. Appendix A contains all of the leadership behavior statements in The Student Leadership Practices Inventory. Appendix B provides a compilation of broad ideas to support student leadership development.

We suggest you read *The Student Leadership Challenge* book, and we strongly recommend having your students read it because we believe it makes a strong addition to any program. However, we do not assume in this guide (or in the *Student Workbook*) that students will have read or have access to the book. Still, you will find recommendations for using the book sprinkled throughout this guide.

HOW TO USE THE *STUDENT WORKBOOK*

The *Student Workbook* is designed to deepen students' understanding of The Five Practices model at both conceptual and applied levels. Each component aligns with the structure of the *Facilitation and Activity Guide*. Each practice module contains:

- A summary of the practice, including a review of the two commitments for each practice
- Learning objectives for the student
- Clarification of the six leadership behaviors associated with the practice
- A series of developmental questions to help lead students to action
- Potential outcomes from these actions to encourage students and help them see the potential impact of making a personal commitment to take action
- Activity templates for suggested activities from the *Facilitation and Activity Guide*
- Ideas for follow-up, with a final set of tips for becoming a better leader in Appendix B

Student LPI

The Student Workbook contains a module on how the data from the Student LPI will help students understand and internalize the feedback. Instructions on how to administer the Student LPI, including delivering and debriefing the report, are included in the Student LPI module (module 2) in this *Facilitation and Activity Guide*. All of the leadership behavior statements in the Student LPI are in Appendix A.

Personal Leadership Journal

The Personal Leadership Journal in the *Student Workbook* (Module 8) is intended to provide a structure for students' action and reflection about their ongoing leadership development journey. A copy of the journal material is also included in this guide.

MODULE 1
Introduction

At the heart of *The Student Leadership Challenge* is a core philosophy fundamental to understanding and accepting this approach to student leadership development. Some of these concepts emerged from the original research. Others were added over time as they became apparent in the ongoing Leadership Challenge studies conducted for more than thirty years. All of them together define our philosophy about developing student leadership.

FRAMING THE STUDENT LEADERSHIP CHALLENGE CORE PHILOSOPHY FOR YOUR STUDENTS

We have found that students commonly associate the notion of leadership with a position of authority or power. As you explore the core Leadership Challenge philosophy, your opportunity is to raise students' awareness of their own assumptions and challenge them. It is important to confront this fictional view of leadership so that young people will open themselves up to the concept of leadership (rather than of leaders) and look more to the behaviors and actions that ordinary people engage in when they are leading. Anchored from these perspectives, young people can be challenged to think about a time when they made a difference and to think about what they did (actions, behaviors, attitudes) that was central to the positive outcome. Take a look at *their* data, and you'll see how closely they resemble what The Leadership Challenge research has found among people—from all age groups, fields, functions, and countries—when asked to describe a time when they were at their personal best as leaders.

We highly recommend using the personal-best leadership experience activity later in this module. Students' connection to their own experience—the data they know to be true—provides a foundation from which to explore these concepts. Referring back to their own story throughout the discussion of the core concepts can help validate and ground them.

Creating the opportunity to discuss these core concepts is key to a successful Student Leadership Challenge program of any kind. It establishes the perspective we believe allows for the liberation of the leader within each student.

The Student Leadership Challenge philosophy has eight elements.

1. Leadership Is Everyone's Business

Leadership is not the private reserve of a few charismatic young people. It is not a gene or an inheritance. The theory that only a select few can lead others to greatness is just plain wrong. Leadership is not a position or rank, but a responsibility one chooses to embrace throughout one's life.

Consider asking your students:

- Do you believe everyone has the potential to be a leader? If not, why not?
- Do you think everyone should consider themselves as potential leaders? What difference would it make if everyone believed they could be a leader?

One question that frequently comes up from students is this: "If everyone is a leader, then how can everyone be a leader at once? Shouldn't there just be one leader?"

We believe that everyone can be a leader, but that people will make a choice about when they step up to lead based on the values they hold. Typically there is only one positional leader at a time, but this doesn't prevent others from taking a leadership role within their area of influence. For example, a student might not be the president of his fraternity or her sorority but certainly can choose to demonstrate leadership behaviors on the committees and groups that are part of that larger organization. They may not be an officer in student government or the captain of a team, but they can take the initiative to start a campaign that will improve the quality of student life. There are also many facets of people's lives. One's position as head of an organization is not the only place to act as a leader. People can lead in many different ways in their homes and in their communities.

Consider asking your students:

- If you are not in a leadership position, is it possible for you to act as a leader? What opportunities can you name outside of any position of leadership you hold?
- Do you need to be the leader all the time or in every situation or setting? Why or why not?

2. Leadership Is Learned

Leadership is a process that ordinary people use when they are bringing forth the best from themselves and others. It is an identifiable set of skills and abilities that is available to everyone.

Consider asking your students:

- Who is a leader you admire? Do you think you could learn to inspire others as much as he or she inspired you?
- How would you learn to do that?
- What obstacles do you see that would keep you from learning to be a great leader?

3. Leadership Is a Relationship

At the heart of leadership is the ability to connect with others, understand their hopes and dreams, and engage them in pulling together for a shared dream of the future. Leaders understand that every relationship contributes to their ability to be successful.

Consider asking your students:

- Does a leader need to have a relationship with everyone in the group? Are some group members more important than others?
- How do you build and sustain relationships?

4. Leadership Development Is Self-Development

Engineers have computers, painters have brushes and paints, physicians have medicine. Leaders have only themselves: that is their instrument. Committing to liberating the leader within is a personal commitment, a journey that begins with an exploration of the territory within.

Consider asking your students:

- What does *self-development* mean to you?
- How do *you* learn about yourself?

5. Learning to Lead Is an Ongoing Process

Learning to lead is a journey, not a single event or destination. Students may occupy many leadership roles throughout their lives. Each will deepen his or her understanding of what it takes to engage others, what it takes to inspire others to make extraordinary things happen. The context in which they lead will change, and with each change comes deeper learning. The best leaders are the best learners.

Consider asking your students:

- Do you have something you want to be really good at? How will you do that?
- [If you had students do the personal-best leadership experience later in this module] What will it take to repeat your success and create a next personal-best leadership experience?

6. Leadership Requires Deliberate Practice

Excellence in anything—whether it's music, sports, or academics—requires deliberate practice. Leadership is no exception. Students need to devote time every day to becoming the best leader they can be.

Consider asking your students:

- How can you practice leadership if you're not the one in charge?
- Do you spend time practicing something now? What does it take to get you to do that practice? Can you apply that to being a better leader?

7. Leadership Is an Aspiration and a Choice

Leaders have countless chances to make a difference. If a person aspires to lead and is willing to do the work, he or she can lead. It is a deeply personal choice and a lifetime commitment.

Consider asking your students:

- What kind of leader do you aspire to be? Can you define it in words that don't reflect holding a particular leadership position?
- What choices do you need to make to become a better leader?

8. Leadership Makes a Difference

All leadership is based on one fundamental assumption: *a leader matters*. We know from The Leadership Challenge research that every leader can make a profound difference in the lives of their constituents. To do that, those leaders have to believe in themselves and their capacity to have a positive influence on others. And we also know that to those who are following a leader, that leader is the most important leader to them at that moment. It's not some other leader. It's that leader, at that moment.

That is the individual whom group members will most likely go to for examples of how to tackle challenging goals, respond to difficult situations, handle crises, or deal with setbacks. We say a little more about this in the final section of this guide, "Onward!"

Consider asking your students:

- Do you believe you make a difference? To whom? If yes, why do you believe you make a difference?
- How can you make a difference to the group you are part of right now?

ORIGINS OF THE MODEL

The research to discover what exemplary leaders actually do when they are at their personal best began by collecting thousands of stories from ordinary people, from students to executives in all types of organizations around the globe—the experiences they recalled when asked to think of a peak leadership experience, about what they did when they were at their personal best as a leader. The collection effort continues, and the stories continue to offer compelling examples of what leaders do when making extraordinary things happen. We encourage anyone who plans to explore The Student Leadership Challenge and The Five Practices of Exemplary Leadership to participate in an exercise similar to one used in conducting the original research. It's called the personal-best leadership experience.

> Directions for conducting this activity are below. The student workbook contains forms your students can use to prepare for and complete the exercise.

A noteworthy finding from the research was that despite differences in culture, gender, or age, whether it was in a classroom, a student club or organization, or a sports team, whether it was in a community service project or a part-time job, in a religious or spiritual organization or experience, in the scouts, or on a school field trip, the personal-best stories revealed similar patterns of behavior. In fact, when leaders are at their personal best, there are five practices common to all: Model the Way, Inspire a Shared Vision, Challenge the Process, Enable Others to Act, and Encourage the Heart. These form The Five Practices of Exemplary Leadership model, and three decades later, this framework continues to prove its effectiveness as a clear, evidence-based path to making extraordinary things happen for individuals, groups, organizations, and communities.

The model turns the abstract concept of leadership into easy-to-grasp practices and behaviors that can be taught to anyone willing to step up and accept the challenge to lead. As measured and validated by the Leadership Practices Inventory (LPI) and Student Leadership Practices Inventory (Student LPI), one of the most widely used leadership assessment instruments in the world, ongoing studies consistently confirm that The Five Practices and related assessment tools are positively related to the effectiveness of leaders and the level of commitment, engagement, and satisfaction of those that follow.

ACTIVITY 1.1: PERSONAL-BEST LEADERSHIP EXPERIENCE

The primary basis for understanding where The Five Practices of Exemplary Leadership come from is the personal-best leadership experience narrative. Completing the abbreviated version of the original personal-best leadership experience questionnaire that we present here allows students to find a standard of excellence from past experiences. The *Student Workbook* contains the forms students need to complete this exercise.

This activity parallels the original research underpinning *The Student Leadership Challenge* and in that way helps validate the model for students. It is designed to help students define their personal-best performance or behavior as a leader. Once they know and understand what they do when they're at their very best, they can then work to be at that very best in all that they do. Ask students to prepare their personal-best leadership story using the outline below in order to:

- Help them prepare to describe one of their personal-best leadership experiences to another student.
- Begin the process of learning from their own experiences.

Ask students to use the outline in the "Personal-Best Leadership Experience Instructions" section to guide their thinking. Encourage them to be open and honest. Greater self-awareness will help them grow as leaders. Let them know they will be sharing their story with peers.

They should begin by thinking about a time when they performed at their very best as a leader. A personal-best experience is an event or series of events that they believe to be their individual standard of excellence. It's a student's own record-setting performance, a time when he or she achieved significant success while working with others. It is something against which students can measure themselves to determine whether they are performing as a leader at levels they know they can reach. They are not limited to times they held a formal leadership position. Their personal-best experience in fact may have happened when they had no official authority but chose to play a leadership role within a group, organization, class project, or even family situation.

For this activity, ask them to focus their thinking only on experiences during which they led others toward an accomplishment of which they are very proud. We use the word *experience* to mean any kind of project or undertaking that had a definable beginning and end. It might have lasted a few days, several weeks, a few months, or even a year or more, but it was something that occurred within a specific period of time.

Here are some things to have students think about when they are selecting their personal best-leadership experience:

- It could have taken place recently or long ago. It was when they felt they performed at their very best as a leader.
- They could have been the official leader, or they could have emerged as the informal leader of a group. They might have been a volunteer or even a member of a temporary group.
- The experience could have taken place in school, with their family, or in the workplace. It could have been when they were part of a community group, a club, a professional organization, a sports team, or at school.

Ask your students to answer the questions in Activity 1.1 in Module 1 in the *Student Workbook*.

Personal-Best Leadership Experience Instructions

Step 1
Have students describe this leadership experience (focus on one unique experience) and ask them to answer these questions:

- When did it happen? How long did it last?
- What was your role? Who else was involved?

- What feelings did you have prior to and during the experience?
- Did you initiate the experience, or did someone else? How did you emerge as the leader? What were the results of the experience?

Step 2

Ask students to list actions they took as a leader that made a difference by answering the following questions:

- What actions did you take?
- How did you get others to go beyond the ordinary levels of performance?
- What did you do to demonstrate your own commitment to the project or undertaking?
- What did you do to make sure everyone understood the purpose or goal?
- What did you or others do to overcome any major challenges or setbacks?
- What did you do to engage others and get them to participate fully?
- Based on what you did or said, what other extraordinary actions did your group members take?
- Summarize what you consider to be the five to seven most important actions you took as a leader who made a difference.

Step 3

Ask your students to review their responses from steps 1 and 2 and identify three to five major lessons they learned about leadership from this experience. Discuss these as a group. Are these lessons they might share as advice to others about becoming a great leader?

Step 4

Have students answer the question:

- From the lessons you identified in step 4, what single piece of advice would you give to another individual on how to make extraordinary things happen in their organization based on your experience?

Step 5

Once they have completed writing their personal-best leadership experience, ask the students to share their stories with others in the group. Hearing other personal-best leadership experiences will deepen their perspective on the limitless opportunities for demonstrating excellence in leadership.

Facilitator Cue

Encourage the students to listen to the others' stories and look for common qualities in them—for example, excellent communication, focus, doing more than what was expected, helping people feel part of the group.

Use the Data

After students have shared their experiences and come up with a list of common themes, capture it in some way so that you can go back to it. Later, after they have learned The Five Practices model, you can ask how well their stories aligned with the framework. Ask if anything is missing; chances are good that the most essential elements were captures. This is a simple way to validate the model in their eyes and help students begin to explore leadership using The Five Practices as their compass.

A DEFINITION OF LEADERSHIP

Leadership is the art of mobilizing others to want to struggle for shared aspirations.

The academic literature offers hundreds of different definitions of leadership. The research that resulted in The Five Practices of Exemplary Leadership led to the following definition of leadership, which incorporates what the evidence revealed:

This definition embodies all of the practices and can help students come back to a simple sentence that clarifies and reinforces them.

Consider asking your students, "What words stand out to you in this definition?"

Use the list that follows to make sure all the key words are covered. We suggest you display the definition somewhere that allows you to go back to it after you have covered The Five Practices model the first time and throughout the rest of your program.

Facilitator Cue

- *Art*: Ask: "Is leadership a science or an art? They keep talking about all this research and evidence. Isn't that science?"

Although the model is based on scientific research, how that model is applied is the artistry that emerges. How we demonstrate each of the practices is a unique expression of who we are. Leadership is full of nuances that each leader brings and for that reason can't be viewed as a science.

Facilitator Cue

- *Mobilizing*: Ask: "What does that word imply to you?"

Reinforce that mobilizing is about helping people to take action. Leaders make it possible for people to move forward.

Facilitator Cue

- *Struggle*: Ask: "Does it have to be a struggle?"

Remind students of their personal best. Ask: "Was it easy? Are things you really want to achieve in life the things that happen easily? Change is difficult and achieving great results requires change."

Facilitator Cue

- *To want to struggle*: Ask: "Does anyone want to struggle?"

Point out the definition if those two little words "to want" are missing. Ask: "What changes? Have you ever been associated with a leader who mobilized you to struggle even though you did not want to? What was the difference? It's about intrinsic motivation not extrinsic motivation."

Facilitator Cue

- *Shared*: Ask: "Why do aspirations have to be shared?"

Ask if they have ever felt they were working with others who were only out for themselves. Did those people inspire them to greatness?

Facilitator Cue

- *Aspirations*: Ask "What is an aspiration?"

Ask if aspirations are about the present or the future. Which is more motivating: talking about problems or talking about possibilities? Aspirations refer to how things could be better in the future than they are today and pull people forward to imagining more ideal states.

THE FIVE PRACTICES OF EXEMPLARY LEADERSHIP MODEL

Each of The Five Practices logically builds on and supports the next one. How student leaders choose to demonstrate the behaviors within each practice, however, will vary depending on their situation and the people they hope to engage. We highly recommend

Figure 1.1 The Five Practices of Exemplary Leadership

that you cover all five practices, and in order, even if students plan to focus their engagement on one or two practices right now. In fact, the practices are interdependent; none exists in a vacuum.

Model the Way: Clarify Values and Set the Example

Leaders clarify values by finding their voice and affirming shared values, and they set the example by aligning actions with shared values.

The most important personal quality people look for and admire in a leader is personal credibility. Credibility is the foundation of leadership. If people don't believe in the messenger, they won't believe the message.

Leaders clarify values and establish guiding principles concerning the way people (fellow students, student groups, teachers, and advisors) should be treated and the way goals should be pursued. They create standards of excellence and then set an example for others to follow.

Titles may be granted, but leadership is earned. Leaders earn credibility by putting their values into action and living by the same standards and principles they expect of others. Leaders not only talk about the way things should be done; they show the way they should be done.

Inspire a Shared Vision: Envision the Future and Enlist Others

Leaders envision the future by imagining exciting and ennobling possibilities, and they enlist others in a common vision by appealing to shared aspirations.

Leaders are driven by their clear image of possibility and what their organization could become. They passionately believe that they can make a difference. They envision the future, creating an ideal and unique image of what the group or organization can be. Leaders enlist others in their dreams. They breathe life into their visions and get people to see exciting possibilities for the future.

Challenge the Process: Search for Opportunities and Experiment and Take Risks

Leaders search for opportunities by seizing the initiative and looking outward for innovative ways to improve. They experiment and take risks by constantly generating small wins and learning from experience.

Leaders are pioneers—they are willing to step out into the unknown. The work of leaders is change, and the status quo is unacceptable to them. They search for opportunities to innovate, grow, and improve. In doing so, they experiment and take risks. Because leaders know that risk taking involves mistakes and failures, they accept the inevitable disappointments as learning opportunities. Leaders constantly ask, "What can we learn when things don't go as planned?"

Enable Others to Act: Foster Collaboration and Strengthen Others

Leaders foster collaboration by building trust and facilitating relationships. They strengthen others by enhancing self-determination and developing competence.

Leaders know they can't do it alone. Leadership involves building relationships and is a group effort. Leaders foster collaboration and create spirited groups. They actively involve others. Leaders understand that they have a responsibility to bring others along.

Collaboration is the master skill that enables groups, partnerships, and other alliances to function effectively. The work of leaders is making people feel strong, capable, informed, and connected.

Encourage the Heart: Recognize Contributions and Celebrate the Values and Victories

Leaders recognize contributions by showing appreciation for individual excellence. They celebrate the values and victories by creating a spirit of community.

Accomplishing extraordinary things in groups and organizations is hard work. The climb to the top is arduous and long; people can become exhausted, frustrated, and disenchanted. They're often tempted to give up. Genuine acts of caring uplift the spirit and draw people forward. To keep hope and determination alive, leaders recognize the contributions that individuals make. On every winning team, the members need to share in the rewards of their efforts, so leaders celebrate accomplishments. They make people feel like heroes.

THE STUDENT LEADERSHIP PRACTICES INVENTORY

The Student Leadership Practices Inventory (Student LPI) draws directly from The Five Practices of Exemplary Leadership model. Six behavioral statements align with each of The Five Practices, creating a thirty-item assessment. The Student LPI is part of The Leadership Challenge suite of programs, products, and services proven to cultivate and liberate the leadership potential in everyone. It is a comprehensive leadership development tool created specifically to help young people measure their leadership behaviors and take action to improve their effectiveness as student leaders. The assessment is made up of the Student LPI Self Assessment (completed by the student leader) and the Student LPI Observer (anonymously completed by others chosen by either the student leader or the assignment administrator).

The Student LPI offers an opportunity for students to learn about themselves by making a commitment to liberating the leader within, and building a plan to do so. Module 2 covers the Student LPI in full: how to administer it and how to use it with your students and your program champions. All of the Student LPI statements are provided in Appendix A. We recommend you discuss The Leadership Challenge core philosophy and The Five Practices of Exemplary Leadership model with your students prior to delivering their Student LPI report to them. In this way, you establish a context and set the stage that will best enable them to learn from their feedback.

MOVING AHEAD

Once students have completed the personal-best leadership experience and have been given an overview of The Five Practices of Exemplary Leadership Model, they are well prepared to explore the model in depth. Before doing that, a module on the Student LPI will give them data on their current leadership behavior so they can refer to it throughout the remainder of the program and beyond. Their Student LPI data thus provide a baseline for them to work from in developing and strengthening themselves as leaders.

MODULE 2

Using the Student Leadership Practices Inventory

ABOUT THE STUDENT LPI

The Student Leadership Practices Inventory (Student LPI) is a comprehensive leadership development tool designed to help young people measure their leadership behaviors and take action to improve their effectiveness as a leader. It is grounded in the same extensive research as the classic Leadership Practices Inventory, which is used in leadership training, executive development, and graduate-level programs around the world.

The Student LPI is available in self- and 360-degree assessment formats, in paper and online versions. The Student LPI 360 is made up of the Student LPI Self Assessment (completed by the student leader) and the Student LPI Observer (completed anonymously by others chosen by the student leader or the assignment administrator), making it a comprehensive 360-degree look at the frequency with which a student engages in The Five Practices of Exemplary Leadership. The Student LPI Self Online is designed for students and educators who do not want to use the observer feature of the Student LPI 360. Key differences between the 360 and Self Online versions are covered in the "Frequently Asked Questions" section later in this chapter.

Student LPI Self Assessment

This thirty-item self-assessment measures the frequency of specific leadership behaviors on a five-point scale. It takes approximately ten to fifteen minutes for the student to complete.

Student LPI Observer Assessment

This thirty-item assessment provides 360-degree feedback on the frequency of specific leadership behaviors on a five-point frequency scale. It takes approximately ten to fifteen minutes for individuals selected by the student leader, or in some cases by the assignment administrator, to participate in the process to complete.

The Student LPI Assessment provides self-measurement; the greater value in the assessment is to use the Observer feature. This measurement tool collects valuable 360-degree feedback from teachers, coaches, student advisors, teammates, fellow club members, coworkers, or others who have direct experience in observing the individual student leader in any leadership role or capacity.

Who the Student LPI Is Designed For

Even if your students don't identify themselves as leaders, the research behind The Student Leadership Challenge indicates that everyone has the potential to lead. The Student LPI tool is designed for students who are already leaders as well as for those who have little to no formal leadership experience, and it is appropriate in high school and college classrooms, student government, campus clubs, and organizations such as fraternities, sororities, first-year experience programs, community service and service-learning organizations, athletic teams, and youth organizations, to name a few. Any young person looking to strengthen his or her leadership skills in school or in the community will benefit from using the Student LPI to learn how he or she currently uses The Five Practices framework and consider how to make more use of the model when he or she encounters challenges and opportunities.

Methodology Used to Create the Student LPI

The Student LPI was developed through a triangulation of qualitative and quantitative research methods and studies. In-depth interviews and written case studies from personal-best leadership experiences generated the conceptual framework, The Five Practices of Exemplary Leadership:

- Model the Way
- Inspire a Shared Vision
- Challenge the Process
- Enable Others to Act
- Encourage the Heart

The actions that make up these practices were translated into behavioral statements. Following several iterative psychometric processes, the assessments were created and administered across a variety of organizations, disciplines, and demographic backgrounds. (To learn more about the psychometric properties of The Student LPI, visit www.studentleadershipchallenge.com, and for additional research about LPI, visit the research section of www.leadershipchallenge.com.)

Reliability and Validity of the Student LPI

The Student LPI has been thoroughly tested as a psychological instrument and is the leading leadership development instrument for use with students. The normative database is updated annually to ensure that the inventory remains reliable and valid.

Reliability
Reliability refers to the extent to which the instrument contains measurement errors that cause scores to differ for reasons unrelated to the individual respondent. Reliability is determined empirically in several ways.

Internal Reliability
One way to determine reliability is to split the responses in half and test whether the two halves are correlated (associated) with one another. If the instruments were completed by

the same person at the same time, we would expect responses to be reasonably consistent between the two halves. If they were perfectly independent (e.g., half is an apple and the other half an orange), we would expect zero correlation (although in the example, there might be some correlation given that both items are fruits rather than, say, a fruit and a vegetable). Should the halves be perfectly correlated (e.g., two halves of the same apple) we would expect a 1.0 correlation coefficient. "Acceptable" scores are usually .50 or greater, and the Student LPI scales are generally above .75. The Student LPI has strong internal reliability.

Test-Retest Reliability

Another empirical measure of reliability is whether the instrument is overly sensitive to extraneous factors that might affect respondents' scores. For example, might the time of day, weather, individual personality, political or social events, internal organizational activity levels, or something else affect a respondent's scores from one administration of the instrument to another administration?

Over periods as short as one or two days or as long as three to four weeks, scores on the Student LPI show significant test-retest reliability (or consistency) at levels greater than a .91 correlation. However, we would expect Student LPI scores to change assuming that respondents have attended a leadership workshop and are consciously working to change their leadership behavior or have experienced a significant life or organizational event.

Number of Items

Reliability is also enhanced when respondents are asked about an assessed behavior more than once. Therefore, a two-item scale is inherently more reliable than a one-item scale. The Student LPI scales each comprise six items or leadership behavior statements.

Validity

Validity is the determination of whether the instrument truly assesses what it purports to measure and also addresses the issue of, "So what? What difference does it make how an individual scores on this instrument?" Like reliability, validity is determined in several ways.

Face Validity

The most common assessment of validity is face validity. On the basis of subjective evaluation, does the instrument appear to be measuring what we think it is measuring? Given that the statements on the Student LPI are quite clearly related to the statements that were listed during the Personal-Best Leadership Activity presented in module 1 or The Characteristics of an Admired Leader activity referred to in module 3, the Student LPI has excellent face validity. Simply said, the behavioral statements make sense to people.

Empirical Measures

Validity is also determined empirically. Factor analysis is used to determine the extent to which the various instrument items are measuring common or different content areas. The results of these analyses consistently reveal that the Student LPI contains five factors and that the items within each factor correspond more among themselves than they do with the other factors. This means, for example, that the items that measure Challenge the Process are all more related (correlated) with one another than they are with items measuring the other four practices.

Predictive and Concurrent Validity

The question of "So what?" is probably the most important concern for anyone who is helping young people develop their leadership skills. To answer this question, we look at determining predictive or concurrent validity, or both, assessing the extent to which Student LPI scores are correlated with other important variables and measures.

The Student LPI has excellent "So what?" validity, as shown by studies of the relationship between LPI scores and such variables as group cohesion and spirit, commitment, loyalty and pride, satisfaction, and motivation. The Five Practices are strongly correlated with overall assessments of leader effectiveness (e.g., credibility). The Student LPI is not generally related to measures of personality and is relatively independent of personal characteristics like age, gender, year in school, and ethnicity.

For example, in studies of fraternity and sorority chapter presidents, effectiveness measured along several dimensions is positively correlated with the frequency with which these student leaders were seen as engaging in the Student LPI behaviors by chapter members. Resident directors reported that the most effective resident advisors on their campus were the ones who engaged most frequently in these leadership practices, and this was corroborated by assessments from the students living on their floors or in their residence halls. New students on campus who were participating in a three-day orientation session reported levels of satisfaction that were positively correlated with the extent to which their student orientation leader engaged in these five leadership practices. Even the effectiveness of peer educators can be differentiated by the extent to which they behaved as leaders.

Overall, a strong normative statement can be made that those who engage more frequently in the set of behaviors described in the Student LPI, as opposed to less frequently, are more likely to be effective leaders. In fact, no matter where on the scale individuals initially score, to the extent that they can increase the frequency of their behavior along these dimensions, they will become more effective leaders.

Impact on Leadership Development Programs

Is there evidence that using The Five Practices model in a formal leadership development program makes a difference in students' leadership abilities? Yes. A number of studies have been conducted on the impact of leadership development programs. One longitudinal study reported in the *Journal of College Student Development* investigated the impact of a leadership development program in students' first year on the subsequent leadership behaviors those students exhibited in their senior year.* Significant changes were reported in the frequency of engaging in leadership behaviors from freshman to senior years. No differences were found on the basis of gender. In addition, significant differences in leadership behaviors were found between seniors who had participated in the leadership development program with a control group of seniors who had not participated. Results supported the impact of a formal leadership program upon students' leadership development.

If you are interested in exploring the research around the Student LPI, the websites for the Student Leadership Challenge (www.studentleadershipchallenge.com) and Leadership Challenge (www.leadershipchallenge.com) contain an abundance of data on past and ongoing research. The normative database is updated annually and added to the research section on the sites. An online newsletter also provides useful information about the model and teaching tips from users (www.studentleadershipchallenge.com).

USING THE STUDENT LPI 360 ONLINE

The following instructions assume that you are using the Student LPI 360 Online.

> **NOTE**
>
> A paper version of the Student LPI 360 is available. Although the general guidelines remain the same, we have provided a brief set of instructions specific to using the paper version later in this module.

How to Begin Administering the Student LPI 360

Student leaders can take the Student LPI Self Assessment and ask others to participate in this process by completing the Student LPI Observer Assessment.** Observers typically include peers such as teammates, fellow club members, coworkers, or fellow members of a religious group or other community or civic organization with direct experience of the individual in a leadership role. They may also be teachers, coaches, faculty members, and organizational advisors.

The student taking the LPI does not need to be in a leadership position, but rather a situation where he or she has been able to demonstrate leadership behaviors regardless of any particular position or role held.

The Student LPI consists of thirty statements describing specific leadership behaviors. Each is rated on a five-point Likert scale, and approximately ten to fifteen minutes are required to complete the instrument.

---

*B. Z. Posner, "A Longitudinal Study Examining Changes in Students' Leadership Behavior," *Journal of College Student Development, 50* (2009):551–563.

**This can be done through the use of electronic tokens purchased from a Wiley representative, directly online, or from an authorized Student LPI reseller (see www.studentleadershipchallenge.com for contact information).

It is preferable to solicit completion of at least eight to ten student observers (in case one or two people do not return or complete them, for whatever reason), but more observers can be invited to participate. There is no upper limit on the number of observers allowed. It is not necessary to have everyone in the student leader's organization complete the Student LPI-Observer (using the principle from statistical theory about sampling a population). The most important characteristic is that the observer has had an opportunity to observe the student in action and has observed that individual demonstrating leadership behaviors.

The Student LPI 360 Online offers administrators time- and therefore money-saving methods for assigning the assessment to students, communicating with student leaders, generating reports, and working with all Student LPI tools from one central location. In this streamlined environment:

- All assessments can be easily created, tracked, and managed.
- Assessment responses are accurately recorded.
- Scoring is automated.
- Anonymity of respondents is more secure.
- Feedback reports can be produced immediately and are accessible from any Web-enabled computer. Also, different educators can be given permission to access a student's LPI data, which is useful when students are in different groups and the educators involved might use the data to help their leadership development.

Best Practices for Administering the Student LPI 360 Online

These tips will help your Student LPI 360 Online administration go smoothly and help you avoid some common pitfalls:

- If possible, administer the instrument as prework, two to three weeks before the beginning of your program. This makes it possible to have the most flexibility in how and when you distribute the reports.
- Start with an accurate database of names and e-mail addresses when you prepare to administer the instrument.
- Create one spreadsheet for each group of students. The Student LPI 360 Online system is efficient in that it allows you to upload a formatted spreadsheet to set up the assessments all at once. As an administrator, you can find an example of that format on the Student LPI 360 system.
- If you are able to administer the instrument as prework, we advise sending out an introductory e-mail communication before the Student LPI assignments are created. This e-mail should come directly from you and describe what this assessment is, your intention for it as it relates to your work with your students, and what you hope the students will get out of the experience.

- Notify students that they'll receive an e-mail from notifications@pfeifferassessments .com and that they should unblock that address from their spam filter. If someone else is administering the assessment to students, try to coordinate with that person so that your message reaches students first. Clear communication at the start of the process will not only ensure you have correct e-mail addresses for your students; it is also very helpful in getting everyone on the same page and feeling confident about what is required of them.
- Also take the time to clear the path or "white-list" the e-mail generated by the Student LPI 360 Online system, notifications@pfeifferassessments.com, by contacting your IT specialist and requesting this change.

Using the Student LPI Paper Version

The paper version of the Student LPI can be used to do a self-assessment only or as 360-degree feedback. However, there are some things to be aware of when making this purchasing decision.

Using Only the Self-Inventory

A benefit of the paper version is that it can be convenient for use with small groups. Also, it can be given as a "self" only, with students hand-scoring their own assessment if you do not plan to generate feedback reports. That makes this version appealing for workshops where the audience isn't known until the session or if a limited amount of time is available for the session and the inventory cannot be done in advance. However, much of the richness of the Student LPI rests in the fact that student leaders are gathering real feedback, which can be an important step in their development as leaders.

Using the Self and Observer Inventories

The paper version of the Student LPI to be used as a 360-degree instrument can be less expensive to purchase initially than the online version; however, there are some logistics and procedural issues. If you want your students to have an appropriate number of observers, you could spend considerable time and money on the labor for collecting and entering the data.

There are other considerations as well in using the print version as a 360-degree inventory:

- Photocopying paper assessment forms is a copyright infringement, so copies for each student and each observer must be purchased.
- It is preferable to solicit completion of at least eight to ten Student LPI-Observers in case one or two people do not return or complete the form for whatever reason, and still be able to produce a solid report. Many more observers can be invited to participate.
- Be sure to allow more time for students to distribute copies to their observers (this may have to happen by mail). Participants put their names on their own Student LPI-Self and each copy of the Student LPI-Observer form before distribution.

- Both the Student LPI-Self and Student LPI-Observer are typically returned directly to the facilitator to make certain that feedback will be available at the workshop for participants. This also encourages confidentiality for those returning the Student LPI-Observer. We recommend that when possible, Student LPI forms be returned with an adequate amount of time prior to the start of the workshop or class session for follow-up with those who have not returned their own forms or had their forms returned by others.

- You'll need to purchase and use the Student LPI scoring software and manually enter all leader and observer data in order to generate individual, reassessment, and group reports (these are similar to those in the online version; on the scoring software, they are called, respectively, individual, comparative, and combined reports). The reports can be printed for students or e-mailed individually.

- On both the Student LPI-Self and the Student LPI-Observer forms, the information in the "Further Instructions" section on where the respondents are to return the forms should be filled out before distribution to students or observers so that students will not return the forms to the wrong place.

NOTE

The Student LPI-Observer forms are intended to be anonymous. The Leadership Challenge research has shown that people provide more reliable feedback when they don't have to reveal their identity to the leader (and this applies for both positive and negative reasons). The trade-off is that sometimes the leader doesn't completely understand the feedback, especially individual responses that are at variance with everyone else's, without knowing the source. We suggest addressing this issue directly during the feedback session with student leaders. Remind them again that they are looking for the larger message, not the individual messengers.

For More Help

Contact your Wiley representative for a demonstration of how to use the online system. More guidance is available on the Wiley Help Desk and by contacting customer or tech support. See www.studentleadership.com for complete global contact information.

THE STUDENT LPI REPORTS

For the Student LPI 360 and the Student LPI scoring software using the paper version, three types of reports can be generated: the individual report, the reassessment report, and the group report. Each offers unique views that can provide helpful perspectives for individual students and student groups. The individual report is the one we describe in detail.

The reassessment report takes the data from one student's assessment and compares it to data from up to three other iterations of the assessment for the same student. This provides the opportunity to view a change in the student's behavior over time.

The group report takes the data from a selected group of students and provides an assessment of how frequently the group demonstrates the leadership behaviors. This can be useful for intact groups that are exploring their leadership capacity as a group. The group report can also be useful for looking at how a class or organization (club, team) views leadership being used in their system, or to view a cohort of students over time (e.g., freshman year and then again in the sophomore year).

Interpreting the Student LPI Reports

Facilitator Cue

If you are using the Student LPI Self Online, you can use this process, omitting the information about observers.

Once reports have been generated, it is important to help students understand the results and position them appropriately. The Student LPI is not about attitudes or intentions but about actual leadership behaviors. The assessment contains thirty behavior-based statements, each asking about a specific leadership behavior and the extent to which the individual engages in that behavior.

The Student LPI uses a five-point scale to measure the frequency with which students are observed demonstrating the leadership behavior.

1	The student rarely or seldom engages in the behavior. For observers, this indicates they rarely or seldom see the student engage in the behavior.
2	The student engages in the behavior once in a while. For observers, this indicates they see the student engage in the behavior once in a while.
3	The student sometimes engages in the behavior. For observers, this indicates they see the student engage in the behavior sometimes.
4	The student engages in the behavior often. For observers, this indicates they see the student engage in the behavior often.
5	The student engages in the behavior very frequently. For observers, this indicates they see the student engage in the behavior very frequently.

A common question we hear is, "Why isn't there a designation of N/A or 'Does not apply'?" Because the response calls for a measure of frequency, a "does not apply" designation is not relevant. The student should simply indicate 1 as an accurate descriptive response of essentially, "I don't do this." Sometimes students believe they are not in a position to demonstrate a particular behavior, perhaps believing that opportunities to do so are available only in formal positions of leadership. The Student LPI approach indicates that is not the case. When an observer wants to say "does not apply" because "I don't see this person doing this" or "I'm not in a position to know if the person does this," it is entirely appropriate for this person to simply use the response of 1 on the five-point scale: "The person seldom or rarely engages in this behavior" from my vantage point. You can help your students by having them select observers who have seen them in action and have data to draw on when responding to the instrument, although it is still possible that observers may report that the leader seldom uses the particular leadership behavior.

Each of the thirty leadership behaviors from the Student LPI-Self and Student LPI-Observer instruments aligns with one of The Five Practices of Exemplary Leadership. Model the Way aligns to statements 1, 6, 11, 16, 21, and 26. These are the statements that relate to behaviors involved in Model the Way, such as clarifying values and setting an example. Statements 2, 7, 12, 17, 22, and 27 align with Inspire a Shared Vision, which involves envisioning the future and enlisting the support of others. Statements 3, 8, 13, 18, 23, and 28 align with Challenge the Process, which involves searching for opportunities, experimenting, and learning from mistakes. Enable Others to Act links to statements 4, 9, 14, 19, 24, and 29. This practice involves fostering collaboration and strengthening others. And Encourage the Heart pertains to statements 5, 10, 15, 20, 25, and 30, which involve recognizing contributions and celebrating values and victories. (Appendix A provides the leadership behavior statements for each practice.)

The Student LPI provides student leaders feedback generated from themselves and from others about how frequently they engage in behaviors and actions that the more than thirty years of research supporting The Leadership Challenge suite of programs, products, and services indicates are the practices and behaviors people demonstrate when they are leading effectively and making a difference.

Positioning the Student LPI Results for Your Students

It's important to help students recognize that the Student LPI report is not a judgment of how well they do these practices, but a collection of observations about how often they do them and are seen doing them. Their opportunity is to explore the report in order to better understand themselves and find opportunities to increase the frequency with which they engage in the leadership behaviors. What behaviors can they do more often that could help them be more successful as a leader? How can they best demonstrate those behaviors? Young people can be very hard on themselves and quick to judge. Your ability to position the report as a development tool rather than a test score is key to their interpreting the results in a positive manner. You can start by having the students identify one thing from the report they notice. If they express it as a failure or as something they don't do well, that's your signal to remind them that this is about frequency of observed behavior, not judgment of their abilities.

Because of the way the assessment works (self-assessment first, then feedback from others), students can build up expectations and anxieties about their results. A helpful metaphor to give them a frame of reference can be, "It's a snapshot in time." Like a snapshot, there is some truth in it, but much more that is unclear or out of the picture. You might joke with them about seeing a snapshot of themselves when they thought, "OMG, I look awful!" or, "Wow, I look great!" It's not the picture that matters; it's what they do as a result of seeing it. Students may need some help in thinking through the emotional reaction they may have to the data.

Another helpful tool for facilitators is to think of this process in the same way one might receive terrible news. The acronym S.A.R.A. is derived from the work of Elizabeth Kübler-Ross and can be helpful in understanding what some students might go through when they review their feedback for the first time:

Shock: The first response to the news one finds unacceptable.

Anger: "This isn't fair, and it's not right!" or, "There must be a mistake!" A common response at this stage is to focus on the messenger, not the overall message. You can remind students of this when questions arise about data that seem out of line to them.

Reflection: With time to reflect, people can begin to understand the implications of the news and move to the next stage.

Acceptance: This is the stage when students understand the feedback and take ownership, accepting that the responsibility to change lies with them.*

Students may need some help and coaching to move through these stages. Here are some questions that people commonly ask about their feedback:

What are the right answers?

There are no universal right answers when it comes to leadership. Still, the research indicates that the more frequently you are perceived as engaging in the leadership behavior and actions identified in the Student LPI, the more likely it is that you will be an effective leader.

Should my perceptions be consistent with the ratings other people give me?

The general answer to this question is yes, although there may be understandable exceptions, which we discuss more when we look at the actual data. People are

---

*Based on the grief cycle model published in Elisabeth Kübler-Ross, *On Death and Dying* (New York: Scribner, 1997; originally published 1969).

generally more effective when their self-perceptions match the perceptions of them provided by other people.

Can I change my leadership behavior?

The answer to this question is categorically yes. Leadership is a skill like any other skill, which means that with feedback, practice, and good coaching, people can improve at it. Of course, few people improve their skills dramatically overnight.

It is important to respect the personal and sensitive nature of these reports, particularly when they are reviewed. First, consider where you deliver the reports. We have found that people need support in receiving their feedback in a positive way. To provide that support, we do not suggest that you e-mail reports directly to students without having established a time shortly after that to review the results with them individually. Students need time to review the report and then immediately need help managing their response to the information.

Ask yourself these questions when you decide on your process for distributing reports:

How can you best support students if the report contains information that is very difficult for them to accept?

Do you have the opportunity to review the reports prior to distributing them so you can be prepared to field questions and concerns that arise?

Can you give the students the reports with time to review them in private should they choose?

Does your plan for distribution and review minimize the potential for a competitive atmosphere where scores are compared?

All of these are options to consider for helping students absorb the feedback in the most positive way.

A Sample Group Debriefing Process for Student LPI Reports

After students have had a chance to review their reports, help them use the information in the report to design a plan of action for developing as a leader. This process, no matter how you design it for your program, has three basic steps:

Step 1: Identify a target (a leadership practice) and a specific leadership behavior students can do more often to make them more effective.

Step 2: Define how students might demonstrate that behavior in their current situation.

Step 3: Students make a commitment to another person to take that action.

There are many ways to do this but each step is crucial. Here is a sample of how you might move through these steps:

> ## Facilitator Cue
>
> Depending on when you are using the Student LPI in your program, you may want to start by touching on or reinforcing key elements of The Student Leadership Challenge and the Student LPI.

- The students have received feedback from themselves (and others) about how frequently they engage in the leadership behaviors and actions that they (in their personal-best or most-admired leader discussions) and The Leadership Challenge research have identified as the practices and behaviors of people when they are leading effectively and making a difference.
- The Leadership Practices Inventory was developed from research on what people were doing when they were at their personal best as leaders. Those actions, attitudes, tactics, and strategies were translated into a set of statements about leadership behavior for the LPI assessment instrument.
- The hypothesis is, "If this is what people say they were doing when they were at their personal best as leaders, then we should expect to find that people who engage in these behaviors are more effective and successful than people who do not engage in these behaviors." Research over the years, now involving several hundred thousand people from a wide variety of organizations, offers empirical evidence to support this view.
- The Leadership Challenge research was extended to college students early on and now has involved more than 100,000 students internationally, from junior high and high schools, community and junior colleges, four-year colleges and universities, and graduate schools. The original LPI, which was developed for use with business and public sector managers, was adapted over a period of nearly two years into a version of the questionnaire that was appropriate for and in the language of students.
- The Student LPI has been shown in a series of studies involving student leaders to differentiate successfully between effective and less effective student leaders, not only from their own personal perspectives but also from the perspectives of their constituents (the members of their groups, clubs, or chapters or the people living in their residence hall or working with them in their classes) and from the perspective of their teachers, faculty, university staff and employees.

Step 1

Have students review their scores for each practice to identify one that might be a good target. Several pages in the report can support this decision process.

The Five Practices Data Summary summarizes the LPI scores for each practice. The Self column shows the total of the student's responses to the six statements about each practice. The AVG column shows the average of all of the student's observers' ratings. The Individual Observers columns show the total of each observer's ratings. Scores range from 6 to 30 based on a frequency rating of 1 to 5 on each of six behavioral statements.

The Five Practices bar graphs, one set for each practice, provide a graphic presentation of the numerical data recorded on The Five Practices Data Summary. By practice, it shows the total score for self and the average of all observers. Scores can range from 6 to 30.

Help students explore all the data, not just their own perspective, and ask themselves these questions:

"What is the relationship between my self-perception and the observations of other people?"
"Is there relative agreement about both my strengths and areas for improvement in each practice?"
"Are there significant gaps between self and observer ratings that indicate areas for improvement?"

When they have made a choice about which practice they want to tackle first, you might use the Leadership Behaviors Ranking page to validate or support that choice. This page shows the ranking, from most frequent ("high") to least frequent ("low"), of all thirty behaviors based on the average observer score. A horizontal line separates the ten most frequent behaviors and the ten least frequent behaviors from the others. An asterisk next to the observer score indicates that that score and the self-score differ by more than plus or minus 1.5. If, for example, the student had identified Model the Way as a possible first target for action and Model the Way made up a larger percentage of the practices represented in the lower one-third area, this might support his or her choice of that practice as a good place to take action.

The Percentile Ranking Page is another place to look for guidance on which practice to choose as a target for development. Explain to students that they can use this page to support or challenge the target choice they have made. This page compares their own self scores with those of the observers to the scores of thousands of students who have completed the Student LPI. The horizontal line at the thirtieth and seventieth percentiles divides the graph into three segments, roughly approximating a normal distribution of scores. For example, if a student's total self-rating for Model the Way is at the sixtieth percentile line on the chart, this means that this person assessed himself or herself higher than 60 percent of other leaders who have taken the Student LPI. This person ranked himself or herself in the top 40 percent of this sample group in this leadership practice. Studies indicate that a high score is one at or above the seventieth percentile, a low score is one at or below the thirtieth percentile, and a score that falls between those ranges is considered moderate. Remember that given a normal distribution, most scores will fall within the moderate range. Give students a few moments to compare themselves normatively with other students. While this is interesting (and often requested by students), point out that this comparison does not necessarily say much about leadership for any particular person in any specific organization or organizational context. Explain by saying, "Because leadership is a skill, you will want to determine what it will take for you to improve your base level of leadership ability regardless of where you are relative to others."

Once students have made a choice about which practice they want to target first, it's time to move them into a choice about which specific leadership behavior within that practice they want to take action on. For each practice, there are two pages of data representing their results for each behavior within that practice. For example, the Model the Way data summary page lists the two commitments of Model the Way and then shows the score for each of the six leadership behaviors related to this practice. The Self column shows the scores students gave themselves for each behavior, the AVG column shows the averages of all the observers' ratings, and the Individual Observers columns show each observer's rating for each behavioral item. Frequency ratings range from 1 to 5. The Model the Way bar graphs also list the two commitments for the practice and then display a set of bar graphs for each of the six related leadership behaviors. It provides a graphic representation of their individual scores and their observers' average ratings for that behavior. Frequency ratings range from 1 to 5. Your goal is to have students identify one practice and one behavior within that practice before moving on to step 2.

Facilitator Cue

It is important to reinforce the iterative nature of this process. Students will repeat steps 1 through 3 again and again as they continue to develop as leaders. If they struggle over several options, reassure them there will be time to practice all of them, but focusing on one behavior at a time is more effective.

Step 2

When students have completed the analysis and identified a practice and a specific leadership behavior within that practice, it is time to move toward defining exactly how they will demonstrate that behavior. Students often find it helpful to share their decision and their scores with one another and ask their peers for assistance in validating their choice and interpreting that choice into realistic actions they can take. Peers often see messages that the recipient of the feedback does not readily perceive. This peer exchange also helps students become more comfortable with openly discussing their strengths and areas for improvement. Going public increases ownership of the data and prepares students for discussions they might wish to have with their constituents.

You might hold small group discussions suggesting that they talk about what sense they made of their feedback. This sort of exchange also helps students become more comfortable with openly discussing their strengths and areas for improvement.

Following this discussion, provide students with a few more minutes to revisit their notes and make any additions based on what they have learned from the small group. They may also have some additional questions and insights they want to bring up with the entire group.

Step 3

It is crucial that you reinforce that talking about what you might do is not enough. Leaders take action. To reinforce the importance of incorporating the Student LPI feedback into their lives, have students work together and make a formal commitment to take the action they have identified within a clearly defined time frame and report back to the others. This accomplishes two things: it helps hold students accountable for their own development and helps them realize they do not have to take this step alone or without any support.

It is also helpful to reinforce the importance of sharing their feedback, interpretation, and action plans with others. Explain that their support will make any leadership development effort that much more painless and any experiments more likely to be successful. Suggest they make a commitment to hold a feedback session with their constituents following the workshop during which they will share what they have learned, declare their target for improvement, and ask for support and questions. It is important to reinforce that they own the outcomes of the experience. It isn't about finding out who said what; it is about sharing what they have learned and asking for support.

Have each student choose a time to hold such a meeting (even if it is one-on-one) and identify who will be invited to attend and participate in the dialogue. If time permits, have students write out what they will say to others about what they have learned, what they were excited or surprised about, what they plan to do in the future, and the like. Tell the students that what they do with the information they have about their leadership behaviors is an important opportunity to put the entire leadership model that they have been learning about into practice.

There are many ways to accomplish these basic steps within any program. Be creative and responsive to your students' needs, but don't skip any steps, and enjoy the process.

Ways to Leverage the Student LPI Reports

There are many ways to use the Student LPI with your students on an ongoing basis depending on your program and your desired learning outcomes. The following are some suggestions.

Connect Student LPI Data to the Personal Leadership Journal

One option is to encourage students to tie their individual report to the Personal Leadership Journal that is part of the *Student Workbook*. When students review their reports, help them identify one of the practices and a specific behavior within it. They can use that to start their plan by defining what they will do to demonstrate that specific behavior soon. The journal provides the format for reflecting on the action they took and the results it produced. Over time, they can track the results of the actions, record their thinking, and then go back to the Student LPI for another target. This approach aligns solidly with the key concept, "Leadership requires deliberate practice."

Use Student LPI Data to Measure Individual Student Leadership Development and Report on Program Outcomes

With the Student LPI, your students can accurately and easily measure their leadership behavior when they begin learning about The Five Practices, and they can use it again later to see how they've improved. If you have your students take the assessment on multiple occasions over time, the reassessment report will help them see the changes in their behavior. It is important that you don't assume that scores will always go up. In fact, there can be an initial drop in scores in response to deeper self-awareness of their leadership behavior and what leadership actually is and the adjusted expectations of the community that is becoming familiar with The Five Practices model. However, the research shows that if students continue to increase the frequency with which they demonstrate these behaviors, over time, their scores gradually increase.

Using the Student LPI in conjunction with the Personal Leadership Journal can also provide anecdotal evidence in the form of stories about the impact a program is having. Research shows that the more frequently students engage in the thirty behaviors, the more effective they are as leaders, and students' stories and some of their data may reflect that trend.

A final reminder: it is important not to assume the scores will go up, and they may indeed have an initial drop before they gradually increase over time. The Student LPI measures only the behaviors of the individual student and gives you a framework for discussion and a benchmark for action. It is up to you as the teacher or facilitator to demonstrate how the program, with all its variables, is responsible for the change in student behavior.

Use the Reassessment and Group Reports

Reassessment Report

The reassessment report takes the data from one student's assessment and compares them to data from up to three other iterations of the assessment for the same student. This provides the opportunity to view a change in the student's behavior over time. It is a useful tool to use in coaching students you will be connected with over an extended period of time.

Group Report

The group report takes the data from a selected group of students and provides an assessment of how frequently the group demonstrates the leadership behaviors. This can be useful for intact groups that are exploring their leadership capacity as a group.

STUDENT LPI FREQUENTLY ASKED QUESTIONS

The following frequently asked questions from students about both the Student LPI and leadership and from facilitators about using the Student LPI may help you plan how you administer, deliver, and process the Student LPI and respond to the questions you get from students.

Questions from Students

How reliable and valid is the Student LPI?

When students ask this question, it is usually another way of asking, "Do my scores make a difference?" The answer, in either case, is, "Yes, there is a positive, direct correlation between Student LPI scores and effectiveness assessments." That is, as the frequency with which people are seen as engaging in the set of behaviors described on the Student LPI increases, so do positive assessments of such factors as their effectiveness, work group performance, cohesiveness, credibility, and the like. Studies show that the Student LPI has sound psychometric properties. (See the full discussion of validity and reliability earlier in this chapter if students are also asking for some technical details.)

Can I change my leadership behavior?

The answer to this question is categorically yes. Leadership is a skill like any other skill, which means that with feedback, practice, and good coaching, people can improve at it. However, few people improve their skills dramatically overnight.

Questions from Facilitators

My students are unsure of what the Student LPI is or what they're supposed to do with it.

We often hear of students who are bewildered when they receive an e-mail asking them to take this assessment; they have no idea what it is or what it is for. As we have suggested, it is a good idea to send out an introductory e-mail before the Student LPI assignments are created. This e-mail should come directly from you and describe what this assessment is, your intention for it as it relates to your work with them, and what you hope your students will get out of the experience. If someone else is administering the assessment to students, try to coordinate with that person so that your message reaches students first. Notify students that they'll receive an e-mail from notifications@pfeifferassessments.com and that they should unblock that address from their spam filter. A clear communication at the start of the process will not only ensure you have correct e-mail addresses for your students, but it is very helpful in getting everyone on the same page and feeling confident about what is required of them. If you're still feeling unsure, there are guides available on the Wiley Help Desk at http://lpi.custhelp.com/app/ or you can contact customer support. See www.studentleadership.com for complete global contact information.

What happens if my students didn't get the notification e-mail?

Often the reason a student doesn't receive the e-mail is one of two reasons: either their spam filter blocked the e-mail from notifications@pfeifferassessments.com that directs them to take the inventory, or their e-mail address was incorrectly entered into the system. In the case of the first scenario, your first communication to them about this should instruct them to allow messages from notifications@pfeifferassessments .com to be unblocked from their e-mail. You can also work with your IT administrator to make sure this e-mail address is white-listed on your institution's server. Ask your students to check their spam folders to see if the e-mail is there. In the case of an incorrect e-mail address, one good reason to send out an initial e-mail yourself is to ensure you have a working e-mail address for each of your students. If an e-mail address is input incorrectly, you will need to edit that token assignment to reassign it to the new address.

Within a course or a workshop, when is the ideal time to introduce the Student LPI?

The choice of when to administer the Student LPI is entirely up to you, but we believe there are many ways to leverage the data in the reports throughout a program and therefore know how effective it is to administer it at the start of your time with students. Many find it useful to do an administration at the beginning of their time with students and then again at the end of the program or class. This assumes, of course, that the time together will be long enough for students to be able to demonstrate the change in behavior. Several approaches are outlined for you in Module 9, and additional ideas are on The Student Leadership Challenge site at http://www .studentleadershipchallenge.com/Resource/resource-curriculum-guide.aspx.

Can the administrator of the Student LPIs be changed?

Yes. Using the Student LPI Online Web-based system, a Student LPI administrator creates a Student LPI assessment, establishing due dates as appropriate, and designates to an individual student leader the task of completing the assignment. Once an assignment is created, administrators may retain responsibility for all administrative duties related to the assignment, may temporarily share some or all of the administrative responsibilities of this assignment with another administrator, or may permanently transfer all future administration of this assignment to another administrator.

How long, if taken online, does an individual student's Student LPI data stay valid and accessible?

If you are using the Student LPI 360 Online, the publisher retains the data on individuals for four years, so pre-post inventories are possible, and you can do the reassessment report to compare up to four administrations for a single individual. If you are using the Student LPI Self Online, the previous five individual reports are stored and can be accessed by the person who took the inventory. More detailed information is available through your Wiley representative. See www.studentleadershipchallenge .com for global contact and support information.

What is the Student LPI Self Online, and how is it different from the Student LPI 360 Online?

The Student LPI Self Online is meant for facilitators who want to introduce their students to the idea of leadership as self-development, whose students may have had little formal leadership experience or don't self-identify as leaders, or who are not planning to use the observer functionality of the Student LPI 360. The Student LPI Self Online produces a robust electronic report, but it does not capture and store the user's raw data.

Should I choose the Student LPI Self Online or the Student LPI 360 Online?

You should use the Student LPI 360 Online if you would like to use observers, or collect and analyze data over time for an individual (class or group). For facilitators who are currently using the Student LPI Self print form and entering the data into the scoring software, the Student LPI Self Online can reduce the time spent on data entry and still offer an electronically generated report.

What is the process for purchasing and using the Student LPI Self Online?

The process for purchasing the Student LPI Self Online is simple and works in one of two ways. First, you can purchase codes through www.studentleadershipchallenge .com or by calling your Wiley representative. You will receive an e-mail with the code and instructions to distribute that will direct users to a website to validate the code and take the inventory. You will be responsible for distributing a unique code to each student along with the instructions for using the code and taking the inventory. Second, students can purchase codes themselves from www.studentleadershipchallenge .com. They will receive a confirmation e-mail with a code and instructions directing them to a website to validate the code and take the inventory.

The process for completing the inventory is also simple. Once students have their codes and instructions for validating the code, they enter the code into the website; set up a user name, password, and account information; respond to the thirty leadership behavior statements; and retrieve a PDF of their report. If students take the inventory more than once, the system will allow them to access the last five reports they have received, and compare their own reports, side-by-side.

If you want your students to take the inventory again at a later date, but you want them to then use the observer functionality and you'd like more depth in data reporting, you may purchase tokens for the Student LPI 360 through www .studentleadershipchallenge.com.

MODULE 3
Model the Way

Practice Overview and Guided Discussion

PRACTICE SUMMARY

The first step a leader must take along the path to becoming an exemplary leader is inward. It's a step toward discovering personal values and beliefs. Leaders must find their voice, discover a set of principles that guide decisions and actions, and find a way to express a leadership philosophy in their own words, not in someone else's.

Yet leaders don't speak just for themselves. They are often the voice for their team, their group, or their organization. Leadership is a dialogue, not a monologue. Therefore, they must reach out to others. They must understand and appreciate the values of their constituents and find a way to affirm shared values. Leaders forge unity. They don't force it. They give people reasons to care, not simply orders to follow.

Leaders stand up for their beliefs. They practice what they preach and show others by their actions that they live by the values they profess. They also ensure that others adhere to the values that have been agreed on. This consistency between words and actions builds credibility and makes Model the Way the bedrock from which leaders can effectively engage in the other practices of exemplary leadership.

FRAMING MODEL THE WAY FOR YOUR STUDENTS

Leadership comes in all different forms and is mostly the model you provide for your peers in how you behave.

—NEIL KUCERA*

Model the Way is about what it takes to be believable and authentic as a leader. These qualities create credibility, the foundation of leadership. Think of building a house. It starts with a solid foundation. This foundation is not the only consideration in building the house, of course; it must also have strong walls, a solid roof, well-placed windows, and doors for access. But without a solid foundation, the house will not stand.

Credibility begins with leaders being clear about the values they hold and ends with consistently aligning their actions with those values. Over time, this consistency helps others believe in them and trust that they will be true to their word. Trust is the leader's currency. With it, leaders can build groups that walk together toward the future; without it, they will walk alone.

---

*All of the quotations displayed in *The Student Leadership Challenge Facilitation and Activity Guide* and the *Student Workbook* are from students in leadership classes and workshops around the world. In their own words, they talk about their personal-best leadership experiences, their most admired leaders, and the lessons they have learned about leadership. These same insights are available from the students you are working with.

The biggest factor in motivating others to join the team was the fundamental personal belief in what I was doing.

—LEAH TOENISKOETTER

Consider asking your students:

- Who do you trust? Why?
- Think of someone you know who is untrustworthy. What does it feel like to interact with that person?
- Think of someone you know who is trustworthy. What does it feel like to interact with that person?

Framing Commitment 1: Clarify values by finding your voice and affirming shared values.

NOTE

Remind students that for each practice, the first commitment refers to their thinking as a leader, their frame of mind, and how they make decisions.

The first commitment of Model the Way centers on the important role that values play in being able to lead others. Leaders must do the internal work necessary to be clear on what they believe in and stand for. They must find ways to articulate their values in a personal and unique way; in other words, they must find their voice because this is what allows others to see them as genuine and believable. Knowing one's values, however, is not enough: leaders also use their voice to articulate and affirm the ideals they believe they share with others. In this way, they give voice to the group and help clarify what it stands for.

Help your students understand that there is no single list of personal values when it comes to leadership. Students may feel as though values like "family" or "honesty" are the ones they are expected to claim, but it's much more important for them to identify the values that truly drive them. Everyone is different, and although people may hold some of the same values as others, they may also hold different ones. This is okay. What matters is being clear about what those values are. Identifying them requires that people explore themselves, their inner territory.

Consider asking your students questions like these to identify their values:

- What do you spend time on, and what does that tell you about what you truly value?
- What guides your thinking when you make a decision?
- Think about times you have been upset by something that someone said or did. Look behind your frustration, anger, or resentment. What does that experience tell you about what you value?

Help students see that even if they are clear on their values, they won't have the ability to effectively lead themselves or others until they share those values with others. To believe in leaders, people need to understand what a leader values and stands for, which can happen only if leaders clearly and authentically articulate what makes them tick. Authenticity is essential: this voice must be the leader's own. Attempting to imitate someone instead of revealing oneself is putting on an act that is tough to sustain and won't build trust or credibility.

Consider asking your students:

- Identify a leader you admire. Why do you admire that person?
- How do you know what this leader stands for?
- Do you think all leaders need to value the same things? Do they need to value the same things you do?

I knew that my teammates, especially the younger ones, were looking up to me and would follow my behavior because that's what I did when I was in their shoes. I had to model the best behavior to set a standard for how to act.

—MATT STEELE

Everything a person says and does reveals to others how he or she views the world. But leaders also represent the groups they lead. The values they talk about need to reflect the collective voice of the group. A leader must pull people together to decide on the values to which a group will be accountable and will use to guide their actions.

Consider asking your students:

- Name a club or organization of which you are a member or want to become a member. Do you know what the group stands for?
- Does the leader of that organization accurately represent the voice of the group? If so, what is the impact of that? If not, what is the impact of that?

Framing Commitment 2: Set the example by aligning actions and shared values.

NOTE

Remind students that the second commitment refers to the actions leaders take.

I learned that those who follow you are only as good as the model you present them with.

—JASON HEGLAND

Credibility is the foundation of every effective leader-constituent relationship. It is earned over time and occurs only when leaders repeatedly act in ways that align with the values they say they hold. That alignment is the key to establishing and maintaining credibility; it is crucial for engaging others. Without that alignment, it can be hard for others to continue to believe in a leader. We've all seen video footage where the audio and video were out of sync: the result is unsettling and hard to follow, and it's a challenge to stay tuned in. The same is true of a leader who says he or she values one thing but then acts in a way that indicates just the opposite. Leaders don't get to be inconsistent with their values. Once a leader loses credibility with those he or she hopes to lead, it is very difficult to regain it. And when organizations stay true to their group values over time, they are viewed as strong, well established, and trustworthy. Without that alignment, they lose credibility and respect.

What does credibility look like behaviorally? Here's an acronym we use to answer that questions: DWYSYWD (Do What You Say You Will Do). It is the cornerstone of the credibility that is at the heart of Model the Way.

Consider asking your students:

- Think of a time when someone let you down. What happened? What happened the next time that person wanted to connect with you?
- Think of examples of leaders who have lost their credibility. What happened? Were they able to rebuild it? If so, how did they do that?
- Think of a time you made a promise to someone that you didn't keep. What did it take for that person to believe you again?
- What do you think this stands for: DWYSYWD? How does it relate to Model the Way?
- Think of a club or organization you're in. How do the actions of the members of that organization align with what that group stands for?

Understanding the main ideas that make up Model the Way is a great start, but remember that the goal is to move student leaders to action. Leadership is a journey that requires time, experience, and continued learning. The behaviors aligned with the practice provide the road map for students to begin their exploration of the practice. We next explore each of the behaviors and provide questions that will help your students identify specific opportunities to take action.

HELPING STUDENTS UNDERSTAND AND APPLY THE BEHAVIORS OF MODEL THE WAY

The strategies and guiding questions around each of the leadership behavior statements that make up The Five Practices of Exemplary Leadership can help you in developing your students as leaders. The statements listed are the same behaviors that are in the Student Leadership Practices Inventory.* We recommend having your students complete the Student LPI so that they can see how frequently they already exhibit these behaviors and which of them they want most to focus on.

Use these ideas to help your students understand their leadership behavior and then apply it. You can work with them to focus specifically on one area to work on to develop

---

*This discussion does not present the behavior statements from the Student LPI in the order that they appear in the instrument. For developmental purposes, we decided that this was a better order in which to consider each of the essential behaviors associated with the leadership practice of Model the Way. This same consideration was applied in each of the following four modules.

a greater frequency of their leadership behavior. Focusing on all six of the behavior statements for Model the Way helps students increase the frequency of their behavior for this practice.

> **NOTE**
>
> For each behavior, you will find two iterations of the statement that describes the behavior: the statement as it appears in the Student LPI and the way the behavior is described in the student report generated from taking the Student LPI.

Model the Way Behavior Statements

> "I talk about my values and the principles that guide my actions." (*Student LPI Report:* "Talks about values and principles.")

We hear leaders talk about how others know what is important to them. When asked how they know, leaders too often say, "They know me." This is much too simplistic! Groups want to know what their leader stands for, and one way they determine this is through the leader's ability to talk about that. The values that the leader talks about become the compass for the group. They are what will guide the group and the members in their daily work.

If a leader isn't communicating about his or her values and what is important, the group can go only by what they see the leader do. This is how they will judge the leader's credibility. And if the leader doesn't share his or her values, the group won't be inclined to talk about what is important to them. Without these conversations, groups cannot determine what their shared values are.

Talk to your students about how they can verbally express their values and what is important to them to their group. Perhaps they begin by writing them down so they can play around with the idea and become clearer about it. Then ask them to imagine having to present the ideas of what is important to them to their group. Talk about what they would say. Can your student leaders articulate who they are and what they stand for? If so, encourage them to take some time talking about these with their group. If not, work with them to clarify what is important to them as people and help them gain confidence in expressing that to their group by getting them to share those thoughts with you. The more they practice articulating what guides their life, the better they become at expressing and living these values as a leader.

Help your students think about this leadership behavior by asking these questions (also found in the *Student Workbook*):

1. List your five most important values. Describe what they mean; in other words, if you wrote one word or a short values phrase, write down the definition of what that means to you in action.

2. Compare your values to those of every group you are in. What is similar and what is different? Are any of them different from any of your group's values that are difficult for you to live with? How will you reconcile the differences?

3. Find three people with whom you feel you can talk about your values. Ask them if they knew these were things you stood for before you told them. If they reply yes, ask them how they knew. If they reply no, ask them what they perceive *is* important to you and why they believe that. Alternatively, ask three of your friends to list what they believe are your most important values. Talk about the areas of overlap and the discrepancies.

4. As you talk about your values, does your language or meaning for them change the more you describe them to others? If so, how? Write your "refined" definitions down as you get more clarity on what they mean to you.

MODEL THE WAY

> "I set a personal example of what I expect from other people." (*Student LPI Report*: "Sets personal example.")

That actions speak louder than words is the simplest way to describe this behavior statement. The key word here is *set*. "Sets a personal example" refers to actions. While we talk a great deal about leaders needing to communicate their values and expectations, they also need to show them through their actions.

If others see incongruence, they won't think a leader is serious about what he or she says to them. Your conversations with students around this behavior statement should be about the choices they make and the actions they take. Do your students do what they say they will do? Talk about this behavior in any context that your students can relate to. For example, you can ask about a time when they might have talked about doing one thing—perhaps being committed to a specific task for a group project in one of their classes—but did something else instead. Perhaps they are leading a group and have the expectation that everyone will be there on time to begin the meeting, yet they show up late regularly. People will watch a leader's every action and from this determine what is okay for them to do or not do.

Another approach is to ask your students if they have ever witnessed a person doing one thing but expecting those around them not to do the same thing. When that happened, how did your students feel about the situation? How did they view the other person? Typically they will say they felt a sense of awkwardness for the person; something didn't seem quite right because they didn't know really what that person was all about or what he or she stood for; they might even have doubted that they could believe the other person in some other situation. What does it mean when someone lives his or her life with a "do as I say, not as I do" philosophy? Typically, it means that over time, others won't be able to believe or trust in what the person says.

Leaders who begin contradicting their actions with their words are giving permission to their followers to do the same thing. Ask your students if they can remember a time when they did something different from what they had committed to. Did they see others begin to follow suit? Did they see the examples they set as a leader play out in the behaviors of others in the group? Talk about the importance of how leaders are viewed in a different light because of the credibility they need to hold with their followers.

Help your students think about this leadership behavior by asking these questions (also found in the *Student Workbook*):

1. List three things you did in the past few weeks that you feel best exhibit who you are as a person, that is, what you value as important. Think about what caused you or made you intentionally decide to do something that aligned with what you view as important to you.

2. Considering the three items you listed, what can you do in addition to those actions that would show others what is important to you as a person and as a leader? Write a sentence or two about the positive impact you have (on a group or on others) when your actions align with what you believe to be important. What do you notice about others' actions when your behavior is more aligned?

3. Write a sentence or two about the impact you have on a group or on others when your actions do not align with what you believe to be important. Think about the three actions you listed in question 1 as being aligned with who you are. Had you instead acted in ways that went against your values, what could have happened as a result?

4. Ask any of the people with whom you've been talking about your values for examples of when they have seen you living out your values. Also ask for examples of times when they have heard you say or do things that are not in line with your values. Define an action you can take to continue or better live your values based on what you have learned.

5. What are three recent occasions when you experienced someone in a group you belong to doing something different from what this person said he or she stood for or believed in (e.g., the person talks collaboration but then excludes others from work-ing on a project)? How did those actions affect you or others in the group?

6. How does a group benefit from members who act in ways that support their values? Describe how a group can be affected when people (you or others) don't do what they say they will do.

MODEL
THE WAY

"I follow through on the promises and commitments I make." (*Student LPI Report:* "Follows through on promises.")

It is not uncommon for young leaders to promise or commit to more things than they can do because there are typically so many tasks, assignments, roles, and responsibilities available to them as members of various groups. Many find it easier to say yes than to say no. However, people who commit to too many things likely cannot follow through.

Similarly, if leaders make commitments to things they aren't able to do or aren't really interested in, the likelihood of not following through is much greater. Either of these behaviors, overcommitting or committing for the sake of going along or not rocking the boat, harms a leader's credibility.

Help your students think more intentionally about the promises they make by talking through what they envision the responsibilities are for a given commitment. They should consider the time a task or responsibility will take, the abilities or skills that are required, the attention that is required, and the impact on the group if they don't follow through. For example, ask them to list three things that they committed to in the past week. Which ones will require the most time, focus, resources, and responsibilities? Talk with them about their ability to meet those commitments. Discuss whether they should make any or all of those commitments, and ask if they honestly can follow through on what they said they will do.

Young leaders need to realize that they are setting an example for others when they make a promise. If they don't keep the promise, they have likely given implicit permission for other group members to have the same latitude in not living up to their obligations. This behavior will generate a negative culture within the organization. Help your students realize that they can say no or they can say yes. But if they say yes, they need to be able to fully commit.

Help your students think about this leadership behavior by asking these questions (also found in the *Student Workbook*):

1. What are the most recent three promises you made to someone else? Did you keep them (follow through on them)? If so, describe how. If not, describe why you didn't keep your promise. In either case, what impact did this have on your credibility with and relationship to others?

2. Make a list of commitments you have made to others in the past five days. Next to each item, write why you made that commitment. Next to that, write how much time (and any other relevant resources) you think the commitment will take (or did, if you fulfilled it).

3. When was the last time you made a commitment that you wish you had not? What was it? Did this commitment align with your goals? What about this experience detracted from your doing something more valuable? Had you not spent your time this way, what else could you have been doing that would have made a better impact?

4. Think about a recent time when you did not follow through on a commitment or promise. Write an action that you will take in the next forty-eight to seventy-two hours to work toward meeting that promise.

5. Think of the last time that you said no to a request, a group invitation, or something that involved an investment of your time. How did this make you feel? Did you feel emotions of missing out, or did you feel liberated by your decision?

6. Think about the commitments you have to others. Are you contributing value in each of the roles you take, or could someone else do as good a job or even better? Maybe you can consider remaining involved with the group in a lesser role. How might this affect your available time and your ability to execute?

MODEL THE WAY

> "I seek to understand how my actions affect other people's performance." (*Student LPI Report:* "Seeks feedback about impact of actions.")

We know that this behavior statement is regularly one of the least frequently engaged in all thirty behaviors in the Student LPI. If you think about why, one reason is simply that leaders aren't always sure they want to hear the answers. Not wanting to hear the truth in and of itself is probably an indication that the leaders will hear things they already know they might not be doing to meet others' expectations. If your students find this behavior to be difficult for them to do, help them look for an opportunity where they can ask others in their groups for feedback on something that doesn't seem too threatening or personal for them. The idea is to begin practicing asking for feedback. We know that leaders must align their actions with their words, yet if they don't ask for feedback, how will they know they are doing this? As leaders ask about and listen to what others see them doing, they can determine if they are coming across as they want to.

Encourage your students to take some time in both their group's meetings and with those they lead one-on-one to get feedback. This can begin with something as simple as asking, "What did you think of the committee meeting last night? How do you think I did running it? Do you have any suggestions for me to make it better?" This series of questions begins with asking for general feedback on how a meeting went and continues to specific things the leader could do to make the meeting better the next time. Part of being able to improve is knowing how one is doing and what to do more or less of to improve. Too many leaders avoid the question, working under (usually misguided) assumptions about how they are doing. By asking the question, they begin to build a sense of trust and a community open to providing feedback to others.

Help your students think about this leadership behavior by asking these questions (also found in the *Student Workbook*):

1. Describe the last time you asked someone for any type of feedback about something specific you did. What was the feedback for? What did the other person or people say to you? What did you do with that information? How did it feel?

2. What strong feelings, positive or negative, have you had in response to the feedback that you have received? Why did you have that reaction? Was there anything in the feedback that you felt was accurate or productive even if you didn't respond positively to it?

3. Describe a time when you received feedback about something others thought you did really well. How have you or will you use that information to help repeat those or similar actions in the future?

4. In your next group meeting, ask three people for their thoughts about how you related to your work with the group. Ask them to describe what they feel about your work. From the comments you receive, write down what you think the main themes are about how others described your work. Define a specific action step to take for one thing you want to repeat and one thing you want to work on and improve. As you take action on these two items, revisit your list of themes and select two more on which you can focus.

MODEL THE WAY

> "I spend time making sure that people behave consistently with the principles and standards we have agreed upon." (*Student LPI Report:* "Aligns others with principles and standards.")

This behavior focuses on the idea of accountability and how a leader can help group members hold fast to what the group has decided is important to them. As the behavior states, this takes time and energy. The leader needs to commit to finding time when the group can talk about and become clear on what they stand for. By doing this, members of the group develop an agreed-on set of standards (i.e., what they stand for above all else) and then determine what those standards actually mean to everyone.

For example, a group might hold authenticity—being who you say you are——in all that it does as a group value. Are the group's members then clear on what is acceptable and not acceptable behavior when it comes to integrity? Do they exemplify this value in actual practice? This reinforces the importance that people must be willing to live by the values of the group. Leaders who are coming into a group that already has defined values, such as a national organization, still must talk about those values regularly as the group brings in new members. Members still must decide that they will adhere to the group's values even if they did not participate in determining them. Whether developing standards or having established standards, communicate with everyone in the group as to what they are, write them down, and make them accessible to every member.

Talk with your students about what they think could happen to a group that either has no expressed standards or goes against defined standards in various situations. Ask them to describe the effectiveness and productivity they think a group can have when they don't know what they stand for. Have your students describe or demonstrate, perhaps through a role play, how they would hold others accountable to the group's standards. Equally important, ask your students to specifically describe what they would do in the case of the group or members of the group going against the standards to which the group has committed.

Help your students think about this leadership behavior by asking these questions (also found in the *Student Workbook*):

1. List the values your group has established. Think about values as both your short-term goals that contribute to the definition of who your group is (e.g., your group might be service oriented, so are you doing things in the short term that are contributing to your group being of greater service to others as opposed to social activities?) and the group's values that your larger goals are based on (e.g., we are an academic-discipline-based group, so do we predominantly do things that promote greater knowledge in our subject matter or is more of our time and work focused on things that have nothing to do with intellectual and professional growth?).

2. From the list of values, name a time when you have talked about any of these and with whom. Ask how the discussion went. Was it easy, hard, comfortable, or uncomfortable for you? What was it like for the other person? What did you learn about how you expressed your values to someone else? For any of the values that are on the list that you haven't discussed in the past month, identify one person in your group you can have a conversation with about any one of them. How does that person think he or she and you (and you as the leader) live up to the value? Talk about how you both think the group lives up to the value. What does it look like when the group does or does not live up to its values? If you both believe the group does not live up to its standards, together write an action you can share with the group to take to improve.

3. Without identifying specific people, make a list of behaviors you have seen group members exhibit in the past two weeks that represent the values of the group.

4. Without identifying specific people, make a list of behaviors that do not live up to the standards the group has set. Discuss those in the next group gathering and suggest actions members of the group can take to better adhere to its standards.

5. Compare the items you listed in numbers 3 and 4. Think about the impact both lists have on the group, and use that to help you lead a discussion in the next group gathering. Use what you have observed to suggest actions members of the group can take to continue to align their behavior to the group's goals and things they can do to better adhere to its standards.

MODEL
THE WAY

> "I make sure that people support the values we have agreed upon." (*Student LPI Report:* "Makes sure people support common values.")

You can help your students work on this behavior by beginning the discussion around their ideas and understanding of what consensus is. Some look at consensus as the majority in the group agreeing on something. Others look at it as everyone in the group having to agree. A leader who is building consensus is looking for things that the group understands and can agree on.

When focusing on what the organization values, what it stands for, consensus is critical. If people don't share a common understanding and agree on the values of their organization, they won't be committed to the work of the group and to each other. This consensus creates a shared language everyone in the group can use; it results in being consistent in how they are perceived and adds to the credibility of the group. When the group agrees on the values they espouse, they are making a pledge to the people they serve.

Ask your students to talk about the values of a group they are leading. If they can't articulate that as the leader, it is a clear sign they have work to do and need to have a conversation with their members. If they can express the values of the group, ask them to what degree they think their group members know and understand the values. Recommend the leader take some time in the next meeting and talk about what the values of the group are and to what degree they accept them. This will give your student leaders an understanding of the consensus the group has on values. If the group does not have a shared idea, they need to take time right then and work on articulating what they stand for. Consensus comes from communicating the values. If the entire group isn't going in much the same direction, they won't be able to get anywhere. Through this conversation, which needs to happen regularly, leaders will help their groups define and agree on their direction.

Help your students think about this leadership behavior by asking these questions (also found in the *Student Workbook*):

1. Define *consensus* for yourself. Ask five other people for their definition of *consensus,* and look for the similarities and differences in these definitions. Think about how these various definitions contribute to or detract from a group in reaching decisions. Pull out the key words or phrases of the various definitions and find the similarities and differences.

2. Think about both a time when you were with a group and reached consensus on something fairly easily and a time when the group had difficulty reaching consensus. How did each instance connect to the values of the group? When the situations didn't connect to the values of the group, share how they did not. What would you do to reach consensus and make certain that the work was aligned with the group's values?

3. During one of the first few meetings, ask members of your group or team what they believe the core values of the group are. Make a list and look for disparities and agreement. Have others describe where the group is or is not living out its values through decisions, changes they are considering, and other actions they take. This is an action you can revisit throughout the year, especially as new people come aboard.

FURTHER ACTIONS TO IMPROVE IN MODEL THE WAY

A list of suggested actions follows that student leaders can try out in order to improve in Model the Way. These are also found in the *Student Workbook.* Some of the specific leadership behaviors in the Student LPI that are influenced by these actions are listed by number following each suggestion (Appendix A provides the complete list of Student LPI statements and behaviors).

1. At the beginning of each day, reflect on what you want to achieve for that day. Think in terms of what you know is important to you and what in your schedule contributes to that importance. You might ask yourself, "How do I want to show up as a leader today?" At the end of the day, reflect on what happened. What did you do as a leader that you are most proud of? Where were the opportunities that you missed that you could take advantage of another day? Can you do anything tomorrow about those opportunities? What other actions can you take tomorrow in which you can lead better? (1, 26)

2. If you are in a group and have a formal, defined leadership role, see how you can work directly with or shadow someone else in the group. In essence, trade places with that person and work on something together. Use this as an opportunity to get feedback from others as to what you are doing related to their work in the group. (6, 16)

3. Use a planner, smart phone, journal, note app, or some other resource regularly to write notes to yourself about the commitments and promises you are making to yourself and others. Write the dates on which you have committed to fulfilling them, and check regularly on your progress. (1, 11, 26)

4. Focus on the little things that your groups or the people you lead are doing. You can become easily engaged in the larger projects or tasks, but remember that it is the smaller details together that help others (and the projects) achieve success. Without micromanaging, look for places where you can make a difference. Think about how you use the smaller things that need attention to reinforce what you and the organization stands for. (1, 6, 16, 21, 26)

5. Keep track of how you spend your time. What is important to you and what you value often shows up in how you spend your time and prioritize what you do every day and over the course of weeks and months. Look to see if you are investing large amounts of your time in things that are not that important to you or that you really don't value. The same might also be said about people and relationships. What can you do to adjust your schedule so that you are aligning your actions more with your values? (1, 6, 11, 21, 26)

6. If you are in an organized student group, visit other teams or groups at your school that are similar to and even different from yours that you know to be considered strong groups. Talk to their leaders, and ask about what they are doing that could give you greater insight in leading. You don't have to be talking about doing the same things to learn and get feedback from how others lead and work. Learn what makes the other group so great. (16, 21, 26)

7. Study other leaders and organizations that you think live out their ideas and values as a group. These could be groups that you identified in action 6, or groups, organizations, or companies that are known to have strong values and demonstrate those values in their daily work. (1, 2, 16, 21)

ACTIVITIES TO LEARN ABOUT AND APPLY MODEL THE WAY

Now that your students have been introduced to the main ideas of Model the Way, some experiential activities can be used to deepen their learning and allow them to experiment with the practice.

Activity 3.1

Values Spotlight

Overview

This activity helps students clarify or shine a light on their personal values. It also helps them understand the wide range of values people hold and the notion that there is no one right set of values. The activity can also be used to identify the values of a group.

Objectives

Students will be able to:

- Identify their top three personal values.
- Understand that there is not a single correct set of values.
- Understand that individuals have the right to hold any values they choose.
- Understand that individuals who don't hold the same values can effectively work together as a group and that the group will have its own set of values.

Time Required

30 to 75 minutes

Materials and Equipment

A list of values (a sample list is included at the end of this activity)
Index cards (three for each student)

Facilitator Notes

Explain that everyone has values that form the foundation of who they are. The choices we make every day reflect the values we hold. Living life in a way that aligns with these stated values creates a foundation for faith and trust. To be consistent in this way requires that leaders know themselves, what they care about, and what they believe in. It starts with clarifying their values.

Process

1. Distribute the list of values and three index cards to each student. Have students look at a list of values and tell them they have two minutes to pick their top ten values.

Facilitator Cue

- The goal is to make the students feel pressured by the limited time allowed. It can be difficult for them to decide because the list holds a lot of good choices.
- If you see students who finish early, ask them to scratch out the remaining values that they didn't select.
- At two minutes, make them stop. Ask them what that was like. Most will answer, "Frustrating," or, "Hard," or, "You didn't give us enough time; there are too many good ones." You can then discuss why it's difficult to let go of a value, but to remember you are looking for the ones that are most important to you.

2. Give students two minutes to choose their top three values and write each on an index card.

Facilitator Cue

- Remind them to think about what helps them make decisions. If there are choices, we usually use our values to make our choice.
- If you are working with a group of about twenty-five people or fewer, it is valuable to go quickly around the room and have people read out their values. The sheer volume of different values read has impact and shows how unique we all are.
- You can point out how many different values are represented in the room. Next, you can ask two or three students who have one of the same values, for example, "loyalty," to write what that means to them in a sentence on their index card.

3. Have all students define each of the values they have on index cards in a sentence.

Sample Values List

Achievement	Cooperation	Empathy
Autonomy	Creativity	Equality
Beauty	Curiosity	Fairness
Caring	Customer focus	Family
Caution	Decisiveness	Family time
Challenge	Dependability	Flexibility
Communication	Determination	Freedom
Competence	Discipline	Friendship
Competition	Diversity	Fun
Courage	Effectiveness	Growth

Happiness	Loyalty	Service to others
Harmony	Open-mindedness	Simplicity
Health	Organization	Speed
Honesty and integrity	Patience	Spirituality and faith
Hope	Power	Strength
Human relationships	Productivity	Success
Humor	Profitability	Task focus
Independence	Prosperity and wealth	Teamwork
Individualism	Quality	Trust
Innovation	Recognition	Truth
Intelligence	Respect	Uniqueness
Involvement	Responsibility	Variety
Learning	Risk taking	Winning
Love and affection	Security	Wisdom

Activity 3.2

Mark Your Calendars

Overview

This activity helps students examine the alignment of the values they claim and the way they spend their time. It's an alignment reality check. This activity can be repeated often and can be positioned as a good resource for personal reflection. We recommend using this as a follow-up to Activity 3.1 where students identify their values.

Objectives

Students will be able to:

- Account for the time they have spent that aligns with their values.
- Identify gaps in the alignment of their values and their actions.
- Define ways to close those gaps.

Time Required

Initially 30 minutes (subsequent sessions may be significantly shorter if they are done as a check-in)

Materials

Some sort of calendar for a set amount of time (e.g., two days, one week)

Process

1. Give students the calendar and direct them to track everything they do for the amount of time you define. Remind them to include all activities, especially those we tend to overlook, like playing games on their favorite device, time watching movies or TV, time on Facebook—all of it.

2. The next part of the activity begins after the students have had a chance to track their activities for the time period you determined.

3. Ask students to get their top three values index cards in front of them (from Activity 3.1). Direct them to review their activity calendars and think about how well their actions (and time spent) aligned with the values they say they hold.

4. Ask them to identify one thing they did that aligned well with one of their values.

5. Ask them to identify one thing they believe was not in alignment with their values.

Facilitator Cue

Give students an example to stay positive—for example, if they chose "communication" as one of their top values and they've just had a clear and constructive conversation with a roommate about doing the dishes. Or if "inclusiveness" is one of their values, did they plan an activity that mindfully included others?

6. Invite students to talk with a partner about what they found and how they could change one thing to be more in line with their values. Make sure they understand that they should actively listen to what their partner has to say. We often get insight from others when we share our thinking and truly listen to the response.

You can also do this exercise as a planning exercise:

- Ask students to put their top three values index cards in front of them.
- Ask them to identify one thing they can do in a time frame you provide that will align well with one of their values. For example, if "health" is one of their values, they can put regular exercise into their planned time.
- Invite students to talk with a partner about what they are planning and why. Make sure they understand that they should also actively listen to what their partner has to say. We often get insight from others when we share our thinking and listen to the response.

Activity 3.3

Movie Activity: *Pay It Forward*

The Five Practices of Exemplary Leadership show up in many movies. This activity features selected movie clips that illustrate the use of Model the Way. Included is a brief synopsis of the film, a description of clips that showcase the practice, and then a series of questions for students to answer or consider.

Movies are a great ways to spark creative thinking about how The Five Practices show up in real life. While the clips listed here are clear examples of Model the Way, look for examples of any of the other practices or leadership behaviors.

Movie

2000. Director: Mimi Leder

Screenplay: Leslie Dixon

Distribution: Warner Bros. Pictures

Rated PG-13 for mature thematic elements including substances abuse and recovery, some sexual situations, language, and brief violence (no scenes for this activity include those elements)

This movie is based on the book of the same title written by Catherine Ryan Hyde about a boy who has an idea for an assignment in one of his classes to make the world a better place.

Synopsis

In the film, Trevor McKinney is a seventh grader. On the first day of the school year, his social studies teacher, Mr. Simonet, gives the class an assignment: each student in the class is to come up with an idea to change the world and put that idea into action. The lesson in this assignment is for the students to think about and figure out what the world means to them. Mr. Simonet hopes to teach his students that they will have a role to play in the world outside of school.

Trevor's plan to change the world is based on an encounter he has with a homeless man. As a result of this encounter, Trevor decides he can change the world by "paying it forward." His plan is to do a good deed for three people, who then must do good deeds for three other people, and so on. The pyramid of good deeds grows as each person pays it forward.

Scene Descriptions

The following descriptions for four scenes in the film illustrate Model the Way. You can view these scenes as individual clips, stopping to discuss each in between, or as a collective sequence with discussion afterward.

Theme: Act of Generosity. Begins in chapter 1 of the DVD at approximately 0:01:50 to 0:04:11.

> This clip shows a random act of kindness between two strangers. The scene sets the stage that leads to discovering Trevor's plan and also shows one example of the impact of his plan on others.

Theme: How About Possible. Begins in chapter 2 of the DVD at approximately 0:07:38 to chapter 3, 0:12:11.

Trevor's social studies teacher gives the class the assignment and leads a discussion about what the idea of changing the world could mean to his students. This scene depicts the students' resistance in their thinking that they can make a difference in the world around them.

Theme: That's the Idea. Begins in chapter 9 of the DVD at approximately 0:31:26 to chapter 10, 0:36:16.

This scene begins with an example of how Trevor's plan has begun to work. Trevor describes to the class his idea of paying it forward and how it works. The design of pay it forward requires each person to do something "big" that helps someone else in dealing with a challenging issue or meeting a need in his or her life.

Theme: Being Brave. Begins in chapter 31 of the DVD at approximately 1:46:59 to 1:50:46.

A newspaper reporter who has been following the movement of pay it forward discovers Trevor's role in it. Trevor records an interview with the reporter in which he describes what he thought had happened as a result of a class project. He describes his reasoning for why people have difficulty changing. The full power of pay it forward is realized in Trevor's description.

Leadership Lessons from *Pay It Forward*

Discussion Question for "Generosity"

1. What examples of Model the Way do you see in the opening scene, "Act of Generosity"?

Discussion Question for "Possible"

1. What do you notice about Mr. Simonet's answer to Trevor's question about what he did to change the world?

Discussion Question for "Idea"

1. What behaviors from Model the Way do you notice in the dialogue in the garage between Trevor's mother and Jerry, the homeless drug addict whom Trevor wants to help get back on his feet in his plan to do a good deed for three people, hoping they in turn will help three more and so on? As Trevor describes his plan to the class, what does he do that reflects the practice of Model the Way?

Discussion Question for "Brave"

1. In "Being Brave," what behaviors in the practice Model the Way do you hear about that were exhibited and held people back in paying it forward?

Discussion Question for All Scenes

1. In any of these scenes, what other practices or leadership behaviors did you notice?

CONNECT MODEL THE WAY TO MODULE 8: PERSONAL LEADERSHIP JOURNAL

The Personal Leadership Journal is available to help students shape their ongoing learning about each practice. Depending on the time outside the classroom or formal workshop that students have available, this tool can be woven in as homework. There are three sections:

Section 1: Intended to be completed once students have had an opportunity to do a thorough review of their Student LPI report. We anticipate that this module may be completed outside the classroom or formal workshop time, though that choice is up to the facilitator. For those not using the Student LPI, this section should be completed after students have a good understanding of Model the Way and the behaviors aligned with that practice.

Section 2: Intended to be completed after students have taken action. It will help guide them on their next targeted action step.

Section 3: Intended to support ongoing and independent exploration of Model the Way.

PRACTICE SUMMARY

Before individuals can be leaders of others, they need to know clearly who they are and what their core values are. They must also understand the values of the group members and the values that their group shares. Model the Way focuses on the values—both personal and shared—that guide leaders and their group into the future. When leaders Model the Way, they consistently align the actions they take with the personal and shared values they hold so that others can believe in them. As we examine the next practice, Inspire a Shared Vision, the importance of a leader's believability becomes even more apparent. After all, we won't believe a message of aspirations if we don't believe the messenger.

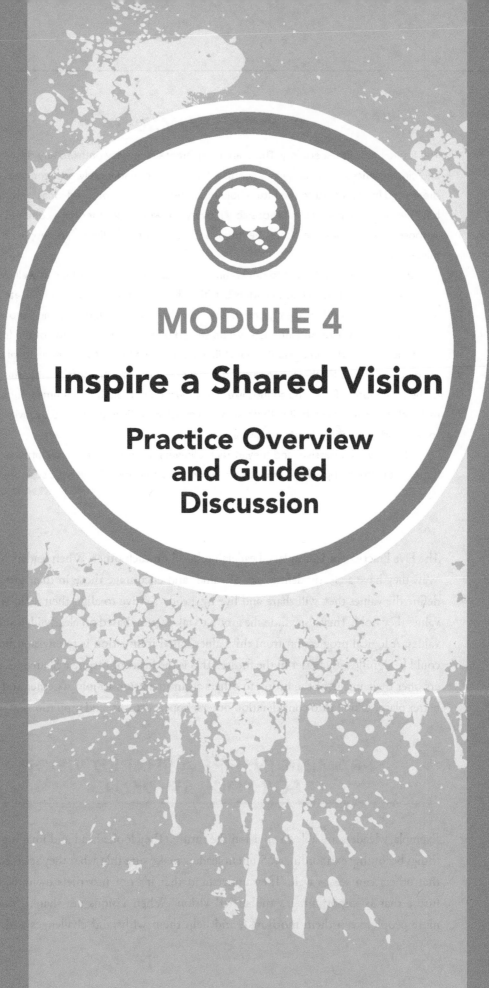

MODULE 4

Inspire a Shared Vision

Practice Overview and Guided Discussion

PRACTICE SUMMARY

The future holds little certainty. There are no guarantees or easy paths to any destinations, and circumstances can change in a heartbeat. Pioneering leaders rely on a compass and a dream and look forward to the future holding in their minds visions and ideas of what can be. They have a sense of what is possible if everyone works together for a common purpose. They are positive about the future and passionately believe that people can make a difference.

But visions are insufficient to generating organized movement; others as well must see the exciting future possibilities. Leaders breathe life into visions. They communicate hopes and dreams so that others clearly understand and share them as their own and show others how their values and interests will be served by the long-term vision of the future.

As leaders start to imagine the possibilities, they must begin to create an ideal unique image of the future for the common good. They must visualize the details: what this image of the future looks, feels, and sounds like. They must paint a picture of it until it looks so real that they can articulate it with passion and conviction. Only then can they invite others to take part in creating this wonderful space.

Leaders are expressive, and they attract followers through their energy, optimism, and hope. With strong appeals and quiet persuasion, they develop enthusiastic supporters.

The Five Practices of Exemplary Leadership build on each other. When leaders Model the Way, they have a clearly defined set of values and encourage those in their group to also define the values they will share and live by. Leaders strive to align their actions with the values they hold. They also guide the group to take action based on clearly identified shared values. A logical progression from this values-based foundation is to envision how things could be significantly better in the future. This is the heart of Inspire a Shared Vision: leaders offer their image of the future to others as an invitation to join together and pursue a better place, taking into consideration others' hopes, dreams, and aspirations as well.

FRAMING INSPIRE A SHARED VISION FOR YOUR STUDENTS

Exemplary leaders are able to envision the future. They look ahead and imagine ordinary things becoming extraordinary. Student leaders make sure that what they see is something that others can see as well. They understand that it's not just their own vision of the future that is important; it's the shared vision. When visions are shared, they attract more people, keep them motivated, and help them withstand challenges and setbacks.

Leadership isn't telling people what to do. It's painting a picture of an exciting possibility of how we can achieve a common goal.
—ANTHONY BIANCHI

A clear and shared vision acts as a beacon of hope and inspiration for all, lighting the way to a better future.

Consider asking your students:

- Think back to your personal-best leadership experience. What was the picture of success you and those you worked with had in your mind?
- What did you do to keep that vision of success in front of people? What effect did your actions have on the group?

Framing Commitment 3: Envision the future by imagining exciting and ennobling possibilities.

NOTE

Remind students that for each practice, the first commitment refers to their thinking as a leader, their frame of mind, and how they make decisions.

For leaders, vision begins in the heart from the values they hold. Visions are fueled by a leader's passion and experience and emerge as a reflection of his or her fundamental beliefs and assumptions about the world: the human condition, technology, economics, science, politics, and the arts. Envisioning the future starts with caring enough about something that it is clear how things could be better for everyone, not just the leader.

Consider asking your students:

- What does the word *ennobling* mean here? What kind of possibilities might be ennobling?

Facilitator Cue

Ask students to look at the root of *ennobling*: the word *noble*. Help them see that this is about having a vision of the future that benefits others, not just them. Also, this doesn't mean that they shouldn't have a dream for their own future. Everyone should. It simply means that as a leader, their goal needs to be inclusive.

As leaders begin to imagine the possibilities, they must begin to create a vision, which we describe as *an ideal unique image of the future for the common good*. They must visualize the details: What does this image of the future look, feel, and sound like? They must paint a picture they can immerse themselves in it until it feels so real that they can articulate it with passion and conviction. Only then can they speak about it and invite others to take part in creating this wonderful space.

The more involvement people have in creating the vision and making it their own, the more support the leader will have.

—DENA JONES

Consider asking your students:

- Give an example of a leader you admire who had a vision of the future that drew you in. What made that vision compelling and exciting to you?
- Think of a time when you've had a "what-if" kind of daydream: your imagination went into overdrive and your dream began to build. What kept your imagination going? What shut it down?

Framing Commitment 4: Enlist others in a common vision by appealing to shared aspirations.

NOTE

Remind students that the second commitment refers to the actions leaders take.

It is great to have a compelling image of the future in your head, but if it just stays there, it won't be much help to you as a leader. Leaders share their ideas in order to open their dream to others. They help others see that what they are doing or could do together can make a difference. The sum is greater than the parts. Visions are invitations to share in an aspiration about the future and make that dream a reality. Understanding the values, hopes, and dreams of other enables you to paint a picture of the future they can see themselves in.

Consider asking your students:

The key was making the vision of our success a joint process because we all came to believe that we could do it.

—FILIP MOROVICH

- Think about a leader who has offered you a vision of the future that you found exciting. What got you excited? What drew you in?
- Now think about a dream you have shared with someone. What did you say to help that person see your dream of the future? How did you express your passion?

Leaders use many tools to make their invitation clear and compelling to others. They use metaphors and stories to connect with others and paint the picture that brings their vision to life for everyone. You know you've heard an ideal and unique image of the future for the common good when your own imagination takes off.

Consider asking your students:

- What was the last story you heard that really stuck with you? What was it about that story that made it stick?

Understanding the main ideas that make up Inspire a Shared Vision is a great start, but remember that the goal is to move student leaders to action. Leadership is a journey that requires time, experience, and continued learning. The behaviors aligned with Inspire a Shared Vision provide the road map for students to begin their exploration of the practice. We next explore each of the behaviors and provide questions that will help your students identify specific opportunities to take action.

HELPING STUDENTS UNDERSTAND AND APPLY THE BEHAVIORS OF INSPIRE A SHARED VISION

There are some specific strategies and guiding questions around each of the leadership behaviors statements that make up The Five Practices of Exemplary Leadership that you can use in helping your students develop as leaders. The statements listed in this section are the same behaviors that are in the Student Leadership Practices Inventory. We recommend having your students complete the Student LPI, so that they can understand how frequently they already exhibit these behaviors and which of them they want most to focus on.

Use these ideas to help your students further understand their leadership behavior and then apply it. You can work with students to focus specifically on one area to develop a greater frequency of their leadership behavior. Focusing on all six of the leadership behaviors statements for Inspire a Shared Vision helps students increase the frequency of their behavior for this practice.

NOTE

For each leadership behavior, you will find two iterations of the statement that describes the behavior: the statement as it appears in the Student LPI and the way the behavior is described in the student report that is generated from taking the Student LPI.

INSPIRE
A SHARED
VISION

"I look ahead and communicate about what I believe will affect us in the future."
(*Student LPI Report*: "Looks ahead and communicates future.")

This behavior focuses on the leader's vision of the future for their group. This can apply to any leadership activity in which the student is engaged. For example, a student leading a class project with classmates will have an idea about what the project will look like when it is completed. Help students think about how they can define a vision in this instance by asking them to envision and describe how the ideal group behaves when working on a project. What does that group look like in action? Have them imagine what a successful outcome for the assignment would be, or what they see the group having accomplished when the project is over. What will it take to be successful? What obstacles and opportunities could come up that would affect how the group functions?

Leaders can then communicate and share their vision with others in the group and listen for what others see as the future success of the group. When students share these kinds of dreams with their peers, they can encourage conversations about how others in the group imagine the assignment. The communication piece of this behavior is necessary to help members develop a shared vision.

This process helps the group collectively imagine the future and provides them with the idea of what is possible. When student leaders imagine what is possible, they work toward that ideal rather than simply beginning to work on a project and hope it turns out all right.

Work with your students to help them clarify what their vision is. For example, a vision is not a list of the tasks they think the group needs to do, a collection of goal statements, or a report of what they want their groups to do. It is an aspiration—something that doesn't currently exist. A vision is a description of *a unique and ideal image of the future* for the common good. While your conversation with your students can be about the dreams they have for their groups, you want to push them to refine those dreams into a clear, concise, and direct description of how they envision the future. If a reply is, "I don't have any dreams about what my group could be," challenge them to spend some time in the next few days asking members of their group to describe their image of the group in the future. As this vision evolves, help your student leaders create a plan for communicating their vision with their groups.

Talking about one's vision needs to occur regularly, so ask your students to think about to whom and how they communicate the vision for the group so that they do it in a way that reinforces the message to the group members while allowing members the opportunity to share their ideas. A vision cannot belong solely to the leader. Talking about the vision with the group and listening to their ideas and thoughts and incorporating them leads to a shared vision for the group.

Help your students think about this leadership behavior by asking these questions (also found in the *Student Workbook*):

1. Describe how you envision your group eight months from now (or a selected period of time that might fit your school year). What changes do you see your group having experienced? What would you hope the group would have accomplished? How do you see your group members having grown through their involvement? What actions need to be taken to make the group relevant? What other significant things do you see changing in your group?

2. What are three things you see that your group will need to focus on in the future related to its purpose? How will you describe to your group why those matter and what the group needs to do about them?

3. How can you talk about your vision of the future with your group on a regular basis? What does "regular basis" mean to you, and why is it important to talk about your vision? Describe the commitment you will make to do this.

> "I am upbeat and positive when talking about what we can accomplish." (*Student LPI Report*: "Is upbeat and positive.")

If you think back to Model the Way and how followers look to their leaders for credibility, which is about aligning actions with their values, it is clear the influence a leader can have on others. This behavior statement shares similar characteristics: it focuses on how a leader comes across in sharing the vision for the group through describing what the group is capable of accomplishing. A leader who is passionate, sincere, energetic, and positive about what the group can accomplish will inspire others to think they can contribute and make a difference. In other words, leaders have to believe in their message. If they don't, others will know. This lack of authenticity can damage credibility, so leaders who don't truly believe in what they are envisioning for the group won't have people following them for very long.

How do your students come across when they talk to their groups? Are they upbeat and positive when sharing their ideas about what the group can accomplish? Do you notice them excited about some things but not about others? If so, how do those differing attitudes affect the reaction of the group to the message? Can you provide some insights to them about the way in which their groups might perceive them based on what you notice? How do your students think their messages are perceived by the groups they are a part of?

Help your leaders do a "gut check" with their groups to see how people are reacting to how they are being interpreted and understood as a leader. When a leader presents an idea, thought, or concept and doesn't appear to really care about it, the group will quickly tune him or her out. That isn't to say the group will give up and walk out, but leaders are sure to lose the interest and commitment of others if they don't talk about what the group can become in ways that make others sit up, take notice, and engage. Leaders are not cheerleaders literally, but they can be figuratively. If they carry with them the passion of a cheerleader, they will send an inspiring message to their group about what is possible. Discuss with your students how their messages do or don't inspire their groups.

Ask your students if they recall a time when they were impassioned about something and their group responded enthusiastically. Then see if there is a time when the opposite happened: the group could not have cared less because, honestly, the leader didn't care. Have them describe the differences and the outcomes. This is a good way to help leaders understand how their behavior and attitude can influence others' desires to come along with them.

Help your students think about this leadership behavior by asking these questions (also found in the *Student Workbook*):

1. Talk with three fellow members of the group and ask them how they perceive your interests and commitment toward what the group is doing. You can ask how they feel when you talk about what the group can do. If they are unable to describe that, use this as an opportunity to talk to them about what you could say to make them more committed and interested in helping the group accomplish what it can.

2. Ask group members what makes them feel good about being involved in the meetings or projects (i.e., what gives them energy and excitement) and what makes them feel drained (as if being involved is more of a chore or burden).

> "I speak with passion about the higher purpose and meaning of what we are doing." (*Student LPI Report*: "Communicates purpose and meaning.")

Whereas the previous behavior statement emphasizes the leader's attitude related to what the group can accomplish, this behavior focuses on the deeper meaning of why a group exists and what it is doing. We discussed in Model the Way that aligning behavior with values builds credibility, which influences how others hear and believe in a leader's vision. This behavior places the emphasis on the leader's belief and confidence that the organization will do meaningful and relevant work and that it will make a difference to those it serves.

As your students talk about leading others, do they speak of the greater good that their groups can provide to those they serve? If not, help them plan out a strategy for speaking with their members to better understand the organization's purpose. This will help the leader understand how others see the purpose of the group, which he or she can then use to better communicate the group's greater purpose. These conversations reinforce to group members that leaders are genuinely interested in and committed to them and the group.

Help your students think about this leadership behavior by asking these questions (also found in the *Student Workbook*):

1. Describe in a sentence or two what you think is the ultimate purpose of a group in which you are involved. Share that statement with the group and see what others see

that is different and that is the same. Talk with the group about how their daily work contributes to that purpose.

2. Using what you found out in item 1, define the shared understanding of what the vision of the group is. Below the purpose statement you provided, ask each member to write one or two sentences about what they do (or will do) in the group to contribute to meeting that purpose. You can have them do this anonymously or identify themselves. Share the final list with the entire group. Is anything missing that you or others need to find within the group that will help the group achieve its purpose? How accurately is the group aligning its actions with the values based on this vision? What do you need to better understand where and why the group might lack congruence? What actions can you and members of the group take to affirm others' values and strengthen the group's purpose?

3. List as many things as you can that you specifically did in the past two weeks to work toward the group's purpose. How did you share or talk about those experiences with others?

INSPIRE
A SHARED
VISION

> "I talk with others about how their own interests can be met by working toward a common goal." (*Student LPI Report*: "Shows others how their interests can be realized.")

This behavior is about articulating the vision of the group in a way that makes others eager to come along. For leaders to engage others, they need to be sure that all group members' interests will be realized by working toward an ideal that everyone shares. To help facilitate this, leaders must know the members in their groups and understand their interests. By getting to know the individuals and interacting with them as frequently as possible, leaders begin to learn about the common ideals people in the group share.

The investment of this time facilitates strong, productive relationships. Do your students know what dreams others in the group have? If not, they can talk to individuals in the group and create opportunities in group meetings and activities to talk about what is important to the members. Ask your students to identify as many things as possible that they believe members find important for their group. If they don't know much about what is important, ask them to have that conversation at an upcoming meeting. Suggest they take some time to learn what members have in common so those ideas can be used to shape a vision or create common goals to work toward.

Young leaders may think of their roles as telling others what to do or where they are going, yet they would be more effective if they were to listen for what group members think is important. Charge your students with creating a list of shared ideas and other relevant interests that group members have that can benefit the group by accomplishing more and making it better. Have them write down how they see these unique interests benefiting the group through actions related to the group's goals and vision.

Help your students think about this leadership behavior by asking these questions (also found in the *Student Workbook*):

1. On a scale of 1 to 10 (with 1 being not very well and 10 being very well), how well would you say you know other members of your group in terms of what they hope to gain from being in the group? Given this score, what are ways you can engage more with everyone or with the few whom you might not know well? What can you do to move your score more toward a 10?

2. What would you specifically ask others in order to learn about their goals and reasons for being in the group? What questions will help you learn about the vision they have for themselves while in the organization? What questions would help you understand their vision for the group as a whole?

3. In your next meeting with an organization in which you're involved, spend a few minutes listening to what people in the group say is important to them. Summarize what you learned from listening to them.

4. Using the summary of what you learned, identify and talk with individual members about how they might contribute to what is important to the group based on their individual needs, interests, and strengths.

> "I talk with others about a vision of how things could be even better in the future."
> (*Student LPI Report*: "Talks about how the future could be better.")

An organization that has a clear, shared vision and an idea of what it is capable of accomplishing will be a better, stronger, more effective group. The capacity to do this requires leaders to define the group's vision in terms of how the group will become better as they all move toward their vision. Groups can't exist solely with the attitude of simply sustaining themselves. If they did, there would be no need for leadership. A group must be inspired to improve. Many young people take on leadership roles because they want to improve something. Tap into that desire with your students to help them think more about the future of a group they're in as opposed to only the immediate tasks of the group. What are your students' ideas about their groups being better or having more impact as opposed to their groups doing more things (e.g., conducting more events, increasing membership, winning more games)? While more things might lead to the groups being better, in and of themselves they are simply a collection of individual measures, not a vision.

When leaders have a vision of how a group can be better, they can imagine greater possibilities to make that happen. With young leaders, thinking of "everything" can be overwhelming. Yet when thinking about the larger scale of possibility, they learn to look to the future more openly. Remember that visions don't belong to just the leader. When they are talked about and shared, others become excited and offer their own dreams and aspirations for that group or project. It is these conversations that lead to a shared, exciting vision.

Help your students think about this leadership behavior by asking these questions (also found in the *Student Workbook*):

1. Think about when you had a conversation with others recently about how the group could be in the future. How did that conversation go? What was the reaction of those in the group? Did they seem excited? Were they eager to start? Were they hesitant? What else? How do you think the conversation contributed to the reactions you saw? If you haven't ever talked about how the group could be in the future, why not? What kept you from sharing your thoughts? If you have had a conversation about how the organization could be and some time has passed, how did this vision influence how the group operated, functioned, succeeded, or was challenged or failed, or changed in some way? Was this vision one that you shared with the group on a regular basis? If yes, how did you do this? If no, what kept you from doing so?

2. Given the impact you described, what strategies can you employ to keep the group focused on its vision on a regular basis?

3. As new members join groups you are part of, what can you and other members do to help them become a part of the group's vision?

> "I describe to others in our organization what we should be capable of accomplishing." (*Student LPI Report*: "Describes ideal capabilities.")

This leadership behavior expands on the statement: "I look ahead and communicate about what I believe will affect us in the future." It focuses on how leaders can share their vision in a way that helps the group see what extraordinary things they can accomplish and what they are capable of as a group, as if there are no barriers or parameters.

One place visions begin is with dreams of the future. While it is common for students to restrict their visions by focusing on either self-imposed or actual external barriers, you can help them learn how to move beyond these walls so they can dream freely. For example, they might say, "We have only six months left in the school year. We can't possibly get this project done." This practice is about the future, and the future never ends. Although there are certain transitions and times when a group's membership changes and leaders change, the future still exists. Encourage your students to work with their groups to collectively articulate what they can accomplish beyond their current circumstances or agendas. Help them imagine how they might communicate to others how they as a group can accomplish something. If a student is still unsure how to describe what he or she thinks a group can do, have this person spend more time talking with others about what they believe the group can do. Greater and bigger dreams will lead to greater and bigger impact and success.

Help your students think about this leadership behavior by asking these questions (also found in the *Student Workbook*):

1. When was the last time you spoke to a group you're leading about what you envision it doing in the future? What specifically did you say about what you envision?

2. Describe the concept of "ideal." If you had a vision for a group you are leading that was "ideal," what would *ideal* mean to you? How close to ideal is your vision for the group?

3. If you haven't had a conversation with this group in which you talk about what it is capable of, list three to five things you think the group can do to make a difference. How will you describe these possibilities to the members? Write out a statement that will help you express what you believe the possibilities to be.

FURTHER ACTIONS TO IMPROVE IN INSPIRE A SHARED VISION

A list of suggested actions follows that student leaders can try out in order to improve in Inspire a Shared Vision. These are also found in the *Student Workbook.* Some of the specific leadership behaviors in the Student LPI that are influenced by these actions are listed by number following each suggestion (Appendix A provides the complete list of Student LPI statements and behaviors).

1. Talk with an advisor, coach, or staff member or teacher about how you might think of some new ways in which you can help a group look at its vision more clearly and about different ways in which the group might better align with its vision. (2, 12, 22, 27)

2. Take stock of what you get excited about with your group. How does that excitement influence what you can do to connect with others in the group? What conversations will help others see the possibilities you can explore together to better realize your vision? (7, 12, 22, 27)

3. Imagine that it's one year from today: What is different about the group? What has it accomplished? How is the group better off than it was a year ago? Why? (2, 7, 12)

4. Talk with individuals in your group about their hopes and aspirations for the organization. Figure out what is shared and how those things relate to what you personally envision for the group. Think about how the group's vision is or is not in alignment with what others in the group think. (7, 12, 17)

5. The next several times you meet or talk with people in your group gatherings, listen for the language they use. Is it tentative or noncommittal, such as, "We'll try," or, "We

could/should"? Can you make sure that it is more positive and committed, such as, "We will!"? (7, 22, 27)

6.   As a leader, ask yourself, "Am I in this role because of something I can or want to accomplish for myself?" or, "Am I here to do something for others?" Are you working to lead the group toward the group's shared vision or your own agenda? (12, 17, 27)

7.   Sharing a vision requires clarity and confidence. If it is difficult for you to talk emphatically and confidently to a group, look for multiple opportunities, such as other student groups that involve public speaking, to speak in front of people no matter what the purpose. The more often you do this, the more confident and comfortable you will be in speaking situations. (22, 27)

8.   Who are other leaders that you find inspiring? Study and read about them to see how they communicate their vision for those they lead. What is it about what and how they say things that stand out to you and cause the reason for your inspiration? Think about how you can learn from what they say and do. (2, 12, 22, 27)

ACTIVITIES TO LEARN ABOUT AND APPLY INSPIRE A SHARED VISION

Now that your students have been introduced to the main ideas of Inspire a Shared Vision, several experiential activities can be used to deepen their learning and experiment with the practice.

Activity 4.1

The Dream Sheet

Overview

This activity can help students think about the vision they need to have for themselves as a leader. We are asking student leaders to think about how they define a vision for themselves, not how they define a vision for the group.

Facilitator Note

The questions posed in this activity help students formulate a vision of themselves as effective leaders. Inspire a Shared Vision is generally the leadership practice reported to be the least frequently engaged in by students. Exploring these questions with young leaders will support the development of a vision for themselves and can also help them as they work with their groups. If you are working with leaders who have experience developing a vision, we suggest that you use the group variation. The questions can be effective in helping leaders work with their groups to determine a shared vision.

Objectives

Students will be able to:

- Reflect on what is needed to communicate a vision
- Develop a clear vision with the ability to articulate it to others

Time Required

30 to 45 minutes (60 to 90 minutes for the group variation)

Materials and Equipment

Dream Sheet worksheet in the *Student Workbook* (Figure 4.1)
Eight large sheets of newsprint and markers (for the group variation).

Process

1. Asking your students the following hypothetical question to introduce the exercise will provide a context about how visions are developed for those who are not sure where to start: "When you see yourself as the most effective leader you could be, what does that look like to you?" This process requires some inner reflection. You can help with a few follow-up questions such as: What would you be doing? How would people describe you as their leader? What impact would you have on people's lives?

2. Have students use the Dream Sheet (Figure 4.1) in the *Student Workbook.* Ask them to write a narrative response to the statement in dream cloud 1.

3. Next, tell them they are going to explore what it might take to get there. Have them complete the following sentences and put them in the remaining seven clouds:

   1. To begin living my dream, I have to experience . . .
   2. I have to learn . . .
   3. I have to sacrifice . . .
   4. I have to risk . . .
   5. To realize my dream I need . . .
   6. Who else can or will need to play a role in my dream . . . ?
   7. What else do I need to do?

4. Challenge students to answer each question as thoroughly as they can. If some find difficulty with any of the questions, ask them to daydream or imagine (disregarding whether they think the response is right or wrong) some possibilities.

Facilitator Cue

The responses need to be related to the individual student and answered specifically about them in the context of how they imagine the kind of leader they want to be. A variation is provided to use this exercise in envisioning a group vision.

5. Using the content in this module, talk about the idea that visions are what drive individuals, and of course groups, to achieve what they imagine for themselves.

Facilitator Cue

Many young leaders have little experience in formulating a vision of the greater future for themselves, much less for a group. These questions are intended to help them begin to understand that by thinking freely and creatively, they can see themselves as a unique and genuine leader. It is possible because they can see a specific path to success and what success might look like.

Facilitator Cue

Since many students are new to what a vision is, give them ample time to reflect on these questions. Adjust the time as you notice students finishing their questions or struggling with them. If you find that students are finishing fairly quickly, you might stop and talk a little about the responses and gauge if they are reflecting deeply enough as to how they are seeing themselves as a leader.

---

6. Once all of the students have completed their Dream Sheet, ask them to share their responses.

NOTE

If more than ten are in the group, establish subgroups of three or four to share their responses.

Reflection on and Connection to the Model

1. Talk about the connection of dreams to a vision. We say that a vision begins with the heart. Dreams begin in the heart too, and for dreams to come alive, they need reflection and nurturing.
2. Lead a discussion about what the students think is necessary to becoming a good leader and how they see themselves actually doing those things in order to realize their leadership dream.

Facilitator Cue

Help students make the connection between what is at first just a dream for them to what can become a clearly defined vision that can guide them.

---

3. Discuss with your students how dreams can evolve into clear visions that are exciting and attainable. Can they see this vision coming to life by doing the things they identified on their Dream Sheets?

Figure 4.1 Facilitator Sample: The Dream Sheet

Dreaming Leads to Your Vision

If you could dream anything about becoming an effective leader, what would it be?

Use this dream sheet to write down your dreams for yourself as a leader. Use dream cloud 1 to define what kind of a leader you want to become. What would it look like? What would you be doing? Then use the other dream clouds to define how you might begin working toward this. What do you need to do to learn, experience, risk, or sacrifice to make your dream, your vision, come to life?

1 My dream of what I would look like as a LEADER is...

To begin living my dream, I have to EXPERIENCE...

I have to SACRIFICE...

I have to LEARN...

Sample—NOT reproducible

Dreaming Leads to Vision

If you saw yourself as the most EFFECTIVE LEADER you could be, what would that look like?

To REALIZE my dream I need...

Who ELSE can I/will I need to play a role in my dream...?

What else do I NEED TO DO...?

I have to RISK...

4. Discuss with your students the ideas and behaviors that might need to change in order to achieve their vision.

5. Have students share their responses. If you are working with individuals from the same group, look for commonalities and ask if those might relate to an emerging vision for the group.

Variation for Discussing a Group Vision

You can adapt this exercise from a vision an individual has for himself or herself as an effective leader to a vision a student group or organization might have. The statements change slightly and are listed below. Feel free to adapt any of them if there are unique circumstances or characteristics of the student group. You may facilitate this in one of two ways as described in versions 1 and 2.

Facilitator Cue

If you have conducted the Dream Sheet for individuals, discuss how this process for an individual leader might be played out in a group setting. See if students can relate what they see as the vision of themselves as an effective leader to the process that a group needs to engage in to define their collective vision.

Version 1: Shared Group

The activity is conducted within the group as a whole. Create a version of the Dream Sheet that is large enough for everyone to write on. You can draw one cloud on each sheet of newsprint and place the clouds around the room. Have the entire group begin with the question, "Our dream of what we as a group would look like as an exceptional group is . . ." and then work their way around the next seven clouds together.

Version 2: Individual to Shared Group

In this variation, have students complete their own Dream Sheets as described in the individual process. Place the large newsprint sheets around the room as described in version 1. Ask everyone to go to each large cloud and write their comments on the clouds. Summarize what all have written, and identify the shared ideas and thoughts. This version allows students to respond with their own thoughts without being persuaded by others as in the shared group version.

Facilitator Cue

Replace the eight statements on the Dream Sheet (see the facilitator sample in figure 4.1) with the following statements to use this exercise for a group that wants to define its vision.

Group Questions

1. Our dream of what we, as a group, would look like as an *exceptional group* is . . .
2. For our group to begin living our dream, we have to create or involve ourselves in the following *experiences* . . .
3. As a group, to achieve our dream, we will have to *sacrifice* . . .
4. As a group, the new things we will have to *learn* to achieve our dream are . . .
5. To *realize* our dream we will also need . . .
6. We will have to *risk* . . .
7. What other *groups or individuals* can we seek out who can play a role in our dream?
8. What else do we *need to do*?

Activity 4.2

Come Join Me on Vacation

Overview

This activity helps students practice engaging others with their vision of the future. The notion of creating a compelling vision—that inspires and drives people to action—can seem daunting. This activity helps them see that they have the basic skills to create a compelling vision and that to be successful, they need only to work to understand others and practice, practice, practice.

Objectives

Students will be able to:

- Articulate a desirable image of the future for others
- Understand that their vision began from their own heart, passion, and values and then connected to the values and passions of others

Time Required

The shortest amount of time to do this exercise is 15 minutes. If you put students into groups of more than two, you will need to increase the time. Estimate 5 minutes to prepare and then 3 to 5 minutes for presenting the vision and getting feedback.

Materials

Paper and pen for taking notes

Process

1. Ask students to think about a place where they have gone on vacation and would love to return to with their friends.
2. Ask them to close their eyes and think about this place. What do they feel, hear, taste, or smell? What makes them want to smile? Have them open their eyes and take some short notes about what they experienced.

3. Direct students to invite the person they are partnered with (or a small group) to spend time with them at this vacation place. Tell them to both think about the people they are speaking to and to recall the experience they thought of to see if they can get their partner to want to vacation in this place. (3 to 5 minutes)

4. For feedback, direct the students being invited to describe what they found appealing in the student's description. Do they want to visit this place? What drew them in? What didn't appeal to them?

5. Rotate through each person.

Debriefing Questions

- Ask one or two students from the group to talk about what made the vision compelling.

- Ask one or two students from the group about the insight into the other person that they used in describing their vision—for example, did they know the person loved to swim and therefore focused on the beautiful water at the vacation spot?

- Ask them to think about how they could incorporate that kind of information into an ideal and unique image of the future of the group or organization they want to lead.

Activity 4.3

Movie Activity: *Invictus*

The Five Practices of Exemplary Leadership show up in many movies. This activity features selected clips that illustrate the use of Inspire a Shared Vision. Included is a brief synopsis of the film, a description of the clips that showcase the practice, and then a series of questions for students to answer or consider.

Movies are a great way to spark creative thinking about how The Five Practices show up in real life. While the clips listed here are clear examples of Inspire a Shared Vision, look for examples of any of the other practices or leadership behaviors.

Movie

2009. Director: Clint Eastwood
Screenplay: Anthony Peckham
Distribution: Warner Bros. Pictures
Rated PG-13 for brief strong language (this element is not in the scenes in this activity)

This movie is based on a book written by John Carlin, *Playing the Enemy*, about Nelson Mandela's work in his first year as president of South Africa to unite the country in the wake of apartheid.

Synopsis

Invictus is based on a true story about Nelson Mandela a few years after his release from his twenty-six-year imprisonment. Elected president of South Africa in 1994, he has a tremendous challenge as he tries to heal and unite a country after years of apartheid. He decides to take advantage of the upcoming 1995 Rugby World Cup that South Africa is hosting and hopes to draw people together through the universally understood language of sport. The South Africa Springboks have less than a year to prepare for the World Cup and are playing in the World Cup only because they are the host nation. The mostly white team has long been a symbol of the racial division and hatred in the country, which makes its ability to serve as the catalyst for country unity even more challenging. President Mandela hopes he can engage the captain of the team, François Pienaar, so that he can lead the team to a World Cup victory, thus helping the country to unite. This film tells the story of how, even in times of great conflict and struggle, leaders who have a clear vision and drive to make things better do make a difference.

Scene Descriptions

The following two scene descriptions illustrate Inspire a Shared Vision. You can view these scenes as individual clips, stopping to discuss them in between, or as a collective sequence with discussion afterward.

Theme: Look to the Future. Begins in chapter 3 of the DVD at approximately 0:08:24 to 0:11:53.

In this scene depicting the first time President Mandela addresses the staff of the president's office after his election, he shares his observation that many from the previous administration are packing their offices in preparation to leave as he takes office. He tells his audience of their right to make that choice; however, he hopes they will stay and help serve the country. The president describes what he needs and expects of those who stay and tells of the importance and necessity of their work.

Theme: Need to Exceed. Begins in chapter 10 of the DVD at approximately 0:45:29 to 0:51:16. Begin a chapter earlier to set the context for the scene.

President Mandela has invited the captain of South Africa's rugby team, François Pienaar, to his office for tea. He talks with François about his philosophy on leadership and how he tries to get others to do their best. He talks about inspiration and what it should do. President Mandela shares how he survived his prison confinement. This scene shows how two different leaders create their visions for those they lead.

In a follow-up scene after his visit with the president, François shares his vision with the team. His inspiration and clarity from the president's message is evident when he tells the team, "Times change and we need to change as well."

Leadership Lessons from *Invictus*
Discussion Questions for "Look to the Future"
1. What examples of Inspire a Shared Vision do you see in this scene?
2. If you were on the president's staff, how do you think you would have felt after hearing his message? What parts of his message stood out to you?

Discussion Questions for "Need to Exceed"

1. When President Mandela spoke with François in his office and asked about his philosophy of leadership, how do you see his vision for the country coming across in what he hopes François can achieve through rugby and the World Cup? What else did you notice the president doing?

2. How does François' follow-up meeting with the team mirror the challenges that President Mandela faces with the country? What do you see François doing to share his vision?

Discussion Question for Both Scenes

1. What other practices and leadership behaviors did you notice in these scenes?

CONNECTING INSPIRE A SHARED VISION TO MODULE 8: PERSONAL LEADERSHIP JOURNAL

The Personal Leadership Journal is available to help students shape their ongoing learning about each practice. Depending on the time outside the classroom or formal workshop they have available, this tool can be woven in as homework. There are three sections:

Section 1: Intended to be completed once students have had an opportunity to do a thorough review of their Student LPI report. We anticipated that this module would be used outside the classroom or formal workshop time, but this is not required. For those not using the Student LPI, this section should be completed after students have a good understanding of Inspire a Shared Vision and the behaviors aligned with that practice.

Section 2: Intended to be completed after students have taken action. It will help guide them on their next targeted action step.

Section 3: Intended to support ongoing and independent exploration of Inspire a Shared Vision.

PRACTICE SUMMARY

Leaders inspire us to move into the unknown. They tap into the values and dreams people hold in their hearts and give them the courage to move ahead together, shoulder-to-shoulder, ready to take on the challenges ahead. Big challenges are an integral part of achieving extraordinary results. In the next module, we explore the third leadership practice, Challenge the Process, and learn how to open our hearts and minds to the possibilities all around.

MODULE 5
Challenge the Process
Practice Overview and Guided Discussion

PRACTICE SUMMARY

Challenge provides the opportunity for greatness. People do their best when there's the chance to change the way things are. Maintaining the status quo simply breeds mediocrity. Leaders seek and accept challenging opportunities to test their abilities. They motivate others as well to exceed their self-perceived limits and seize the initiative to make something meaningful happen. Leaders treat every assignment as an adventure.

Most innovations come not from leaders themselves but from the people closest to the work. They also come from "outsight"—the way exemplary leaders look outward for good ideas everywhere. Leaders promote external communication and then listen, take advice, and learn.

Progress is made incrementally, not in giant leaps. Exemplary leaders move forward in small steps with little victories. They turn adversity into advantage and setbacks into successes. They persevere with grit and determination.

Leaders venture out. They test and they take risks with bold ideas. And because risk taking involves mistakes and failure, leaders accept and grow from the inevitable disappointments. They treat these as learning opportunities.

As we've said before, The Five Practices of Exemplary Leadership build on each other. When leaders Model the Way, they have a clearly defined set of values and encourage those in their group to also define the values they share and will live by. Leaders strive to align their actions with the values they hold, as well as those of others in the group with the identified shared values. A logical progression from this values-based foundation is to envision how things could be better. This is the heart of the second practice: Inspire a Shared Vision. Leaders offer their image of the future to others as an invitation to join together and pursue a better place, taking into consideration the dreams and aspirations of others as well. But to get to this new place, you can't settle for the same old, same old. To move to new, uncharted territory and do things better than they've been done before, leaders must do things differently. They must Challenge the Process.

Challenge the Process focuses on how leaders can make the transition from what they and their constituents have only imagined to considering what actions they will have to take to make their shared visions come alive. This requires not just innovative thinking but a willingness to do things that may have never been done before and to take some risks, experiment, make some mistakes, and learn from these experiences. It is about the behaviors that help leaders think openly and creatively; it is as well about making sure that they help others feel safe to do the same.

FRAMING CHALLENGE THE PROCESS FOR YOUR STUDENTS

Visions are about the future. What you imagine does not yet exist. To move forward into the unknown requires you to do things differently. If you don't Challenge the Process, things will likely stay the same, and probably get worse. Challenging the Process refers to putting feet on the ground, that is, the actions required to begin transforming possibilities into realities. Link this concept to your students' personal best experience. What would have happened if they had only dreamed about what might be and hadn't been willing to do things differently? Would they have achieved the same success?

Consider asking your students:

- Think back to your personal-best leadership experience. In what way were your accomplishments the result of doing things as you had always done them?
- Why did you choose to do the things you did?
- Would you be surprised that this is the leadership practice that most students engage in least frequently? What's behind this finding?

When I did question the status quo, when I did come up with innovative ideas, when I followed through with the changes I suggested, got feedback, understood my mistakes, learned from them, and was open to improvements I won the respect of the people around me.

—VARUN MUNDRA

Challenge the Process isn't about breaking rules just to challenge the system. It's about questioning the status quo with the intention of making things better. The work of leaders is change for the greater good, not for personal gain.

Consider asking your students:

- What are leaders doing when they Challenge the Process? What are they doing for themselves, and what are they doing for others?
- How is Challenge the Process about more than breaking rules? If they were only breaking the rules or proposing changes just to be different, what would the results from Challenge the Process look like?
- What does it mean to you to Challenge the Process? Can you share a good example?
- Why is the leader not the only one who can Challenge the Process? How do others challenge? How do leaders make it possible for others to Challenge the Process?

Framing Commitment 5: Search for opportunities by seizing the initiative and looking outward for innovative ways to improve.

NOTE

Remind students that the first commitment refers to their thinking as a leader, their frame of mind, and how they make decisions.

This first commitment of Challenge the Process focuses on the way a leader thinks. It defines the open-minded approach so key to this practice. Leaders don't sit around and wait for new ideas to pop up. They actively seek out other perspectives and willingly reach into new territory to find them. They do this not simply to inspire change for the sake of change or simply to rattle the cage to see what might happen; they challenge with the purpose of improving the status quo. Their explorations also set an example and tone for others around them to do the same.

Students generally play it safe when it comes to classroom assignments, group projects, and tasks because they don't want to be the one to "mess it up." They worry about failure and how it might harm their individual reputation or record. That fear extends to being willing to do everything themselves rather than risk relying on others, and vice versa. But one definition of insanity is doing the same thing over and over and expecting a different result. It makes sense, then, that if students want to achieve an extraordinarily unusual result, they have to be willing to explore different ways to approach it and new ways to achieve it. In some cases, this also means raising their aspirational levels (e.g., "getting a passing grade is not good enough"). Research shows that leadership is inextricably linked to taking on the status quo and a willingness to be innovative. Leaders are innovators of change and embrace the uncertainty that comes with pushing into the unknown.

Consider asking your students:

I learned that in all environments when things don't work properly you shouldn't just accept it as being "just the way it is." There are in fact massive opportunities to shine as an innovative person.
—JADE LUI

- What stops you from trying something new? What do you risk if you change your approach?
- What is the risk if you don't change your approach?
- Why do you need to be innovative to be a good leader?
- Think back to your personal-best leadership experience. What made you confident enough to take the risks and do the work you did?

Student leaders look outside themselves and their environments for new ideas. They use "outsight," which means that they are willing to look beyond their own experiences and consider other perspectives and experiences in understanding what is going on and what could be. This builds their capacity to draw on the "insight" of others, explore new places, and encourage collaborative innovative thinking.

Our goal seemed enormous, so we broke it down into parts and gave one part to each member.
—RICHARD CABRAL

Consider asking your students:

- What does it mean to use outsight? Can you give an example?
- Think about how things get invented. What drives that?
- What do you do to come up with fresh new ideas?
- Have you ever been surprised by what someone had to contribute (e.g., a great idea or a new skill)? What does your surprise reveal?

Framing Commitment 6: Experiment and take risks by constantly generating small wins and learning from experience.

> **NOTE**
>
> Remind students that the second commitment refers to the actions leaders take.

As a leader, not everything you propose or do will work out as you intended. The unique perspective of effective leaders is that they consider these experiences to be learning opportunities. A small win is a step forward; it builds momentum and gets others on your side. Leaders help others see what progress has been made as a result of what's gone right and what can be learned from what's gone wrong. Leaders are great learners and are willing to try out new ideas even when there is no guarantee of success because they appreciate that they will always learn something that will be helpful to them in moving forward. They build on each of their experiences, much the way scientists do, in discovering future possibilities. Doing this bit by bit helps create the motivation for others to continue to invest their time and energy into doing something that has never been done before.

Consider asking your students:

- We look at amazing athletes and think, "They never make a mistake!" But how much truth is there in that statement?
- Think back to your personal-best leadership experience. What happened when there were moments when things didn't go as planned?
- How has someone helped you learn from a mistake you made? What happened?
- What happens if everyone is afraid to take a chance or try something new?

The similarity that most stuck out was that each person's story was about having to overcome uncertainty and fear in order to achieve his or her best.
—KATHERINE WINKEL

Getting people to change the way they do things and take risks in pursuit of an extraordinary result is not easy. They need to feel safe to do things differently. Leaders create that safe environment by breaking down seemingly insurmountable problems into doable tasks. They create the sense that the next small step is possible and within their control.

Consider asking your students:

- Think of a time you felt encouraged by someone who helped you realize that you were making progress toward a goal. What did this person say to you that helped? What would have happened if he or she hadn't talked to you?
- When you break things down into smaller components so you don't feel overwhelmed, what do you do? How does that make you feel?

Leaders also create ongoing small markers of success. They accumulate "yeses" to build confidence and reinforce people's desire to be successful. They make people want to do more, to move ahead and not back.

Consider asking your students:

- Think of a time when you trained to do something new or to perform at some higher level of skill. Do you remember when you hit your first success? What was it? Who helped you realize that it was an accomplishment? What did that person say?
- What happens if you're working on something that is important to you and all you hear is "No," or, "Not good enough," or, "Not yet"? How does that make you feel? What can you do to address this downer?

HELPING STUDENTS UNDERSTAND AND APPLY THE BEHAVIORS OF CHALLENGE THE PROCESS

There are some specific strategies and guiding questions around each of the leadership behavior statements that make up The Five Practices of Exemplary Leadership that you can use in helping your students develop as leaders. The statements listed in this section are the same behaviors that are in the Student Leadership Practices Inventory. We recommend having your students complete the Student LPI so that they can understand how frequently they already exhibit these behaviors and which of them they want most to focus on.

Use these ideas to help your students understand their leadership behavior and then apply it. You can work with students to focus specifically on one area to work on to develop a greater frequency of their leadership behavior. Focusing on all six of the behavior statements for Challenge the Process helps students increase the frequency of their behavior for this practice.

For each behavior, you will find two iterations of the statement that describe the behavior: (1) the statement as it appears in the Student LPI and (2) the way the behavior is described in the student report that is generated from taking the Student LPI.

CHALLENGE
THE PROCESS

> "I look for ways to develop and challenge my skills and abilities." (*Student LPI Report:* "Challenges skills and abilities.")

Most will agree that having better and broader skills sets one person apart from others. The work required to develop one's skills and abilities is more effective when it is purposeful than when it is happenstance. Similarly, student leaders who recognize the need for and take the initiative to work on improving their skills will experience greater growth than when they are constantly instructed on what they should do. Students often won't take the initiative to work on developing their abilities. Quite possibly they have a fear of a new and challenging experience, and this makes them uncomfortable. Trying something new can create some anxiety for anyone. Sometimes it's easier for students to ignore or shy away from opportunities that can help them grow. Part of the reason is the unknown, and part could simply be that they don't want to do the work.

A first step to take with young leaders is to ask them to look for opportunities that are interesting to them. If they can get more engaged and involved in any curricular and cocurricular experiences offered at their school, they will begin to find specific places they can work on skills they want to develop. Talk with them about some of the abilities they might want to develop. Tying this conversation to their academic program, life goals, and career interests will put a clearer focus on the opportunities they can take advantage of to learn and grow.

Sometimes students want to be viewed as knowing what they are doing. They can feel a sense of incompetence if they were to have to work on developing or improving skills they think they should already have as a leader. If your students are hesitant to step out and try some new things, talk with them about what is holding them back. Perhaps they think they don't need to work on developing skills beyond what they feel good about now; "That will come later when I need them," they might say. Maybe they think it will take too much time and they have other things to focus on. Still, skill development takes time. It can't happen in a day, but it should begin happening today.

Work with your students to help them become more self-directed and aware of opportunities they can take advantage of to improve their abilities. What we are talking about here is self-awareness coupled with self-development. Ask questions that help them explore what they feel a need to work on. Help them to think about their strengths so they can continue that growth. But also help them acknowledge the areas in which they can put more time and energy into development.

A sustainable learning environment evolves as students are more connected and find new opportunities to develop their abilities. This must become a lifelong learning process. Talk to them about how new opportunities will emerge throughout their life; when they do, that is not the time to begin preparing. *Now is.*

Help your students think about this leadership behavior by asking these questions (also found in the *Student Workbook*):

1. What are three skills or abilities you want to learn or develop that would help you be a better leader?

2. Where can you find a group, activity, or project that might offer you the chance to learn specific new skills or strengthen ones you have now?

3. Who has the individual skill set you desire? Can you talk with that person to learn from his or her experience? How did this person go about developing those skills and acquiring those talents?

4. How will you evaluate your progress in developing your skills? Who could you talk with who would give you feedback about your current level of relevant skills and abilities?

CHALLENGE
THE PROCESS

> "I search for innovative ways to improve what we are doing." (*Student LPI Report:* "Searches for innovative ways to improve.")

How frequently do student leaders hit the ground running and take charge by delegating tasks, making group assignments, or simply doing the work of their groups themselves? What would the value be of a student leader spending more time to develop a good understanding of how the group operates and what circumstances or situations influence its purpose and work? Even with the simplest of organizations and groups, many other variables can be assets to or hindrances for the group. Student leaders who can take stock of what is going on within and around their groups and apply that learning will better be able to identify opportunities for learning and trying new things.

For groups, getting stuck can be particularly difficult. Group members trying to create a new program or solve a problem might find themselves struggling, not being sure what to do or what to try next. If leaders work to stay current on what is going on, they discover new opportunities to learn. Even for the simplest of student groups, there are events, situations, and circumstances that affect what the group is doing or can do. Leaders need to work to make themselves aware of the events and circumstances so they can learn and apply what they have discovered to help their groups improve.

Help your students think about this leadership behavior by asking these questions (also found in the *Student Workbook*):

1. Ask your group to identify three things they think get in the way of their ability to be even more successful. Come up with some actions the group can take to address those inhibitors.

2. Taking the responses from the previous question, look for other groups at your school or a similar organization that you think do those things well. Spend time talking with others in those groups to learn what they do in similar circumstances. Find out how they overcame their obstacles and discuss with your colleagues how your group can use those lessons learned.

3. State the specific actions you will take to help your group implement what you learned about other groups to overcome obstacles the group or your group is facing.

> "I take initiative in experimenting with the way things can be done." (*Student LPI Report:* "Takes initiative in experimenting.")

Risk taking can be, well, risky. Some young leaders who take a risk and find that it doesn't quite work out rarely step out again. They don't want to be seen as the one who failed or messed up. Yet trying new possibilities is how we know things get better.

Two key actions in this behavior stand out: initiative and experimenting. The former requires being assertive, and the latter includes having a level of confidence or at least a capacity or willingness for trying new things. When students find new opportunities, they have to act on them by taking the initiative to do something and then having the courage to try something new. If they are dealing with something their groups have been struggling with, never quite moving in a better direction, then they will have to do something new to try and get unstuck.

We know that in most situations young leaders face, there is little detrimental risk. And most education or youth development environments are great places for younger leaders to try new things with little risk of significant consequences. This behavior in a supportive environment is a great place for young leaders to develop the confidence to experiment with ways to move a group forward.

Help your students think about this leadership behavior by asking these questions (also found in the *Student Workbook*):

1. What would it take for you to help your group feel comfortable about trying something new?

2. In what activity could you encourage your group to do something different from what they have done in the past that would improve the activity?

3. How can you help others feel safe in expressing their ideas for trying something new?

4. What statements or language can you encourage your group to remove from their vocabulary that will enable them to try a new experiment?

> "I make sure that big projects we undertake are broken down into smaller and doable parts." (*Student LPI Report:* "Breaks projects into smaller doable portions.")

Similar to the issues related to searching outside the organization for innovative ways to improve, it might be all too common for student leaders to jump right in and begin working with their group on the daily demands without a specific plan or set goals in place. Setting daily, weekly, monthly, and even semester-long or annual goals gives groups the direction they need to succeed in achieving their aspirations.

Leaders must hold their groups accountable to themselves by having them define their targets. This might seem tedious at times; nonetheless, effective leaders lead discussions and processes that push the group to set achievable milestones through specific and intentional planning. This investment on the front end will be important to the group's success throughout its work.

Help your students think about this leadership behavior by asking these questions (also found in the *Student Workbook*):

1. What are three pieces of a large project for which you can establish milestones with your group to meet in the upcoming _____ (describe the time frames for any or all of the portions of the project that best suit your group's meeting and work schedules)?

Week

1.

2.

3.

Month

1.

2.

3.

Quarter/Semester

1.

2.

3.

Academic Year

1.

2.

3.

2. How will you help your group determine if these milestones were met? If you do meet them, do you know what you did for that to happen? If you don't meet them, do you know what caused that?
3. Identify a new project, area, or initiative the group will work on and set a reasonable number of goals for that activity. Follow the same process as listed in items 2 and 3 to determine your progress toward meeting your goals. As you see the group grow, extend the goals.

CHALLENGE
THE PROCESS

> "I look for ways that others can try out new ideas and methods." (Student LPI Report: "Helps others try out new ideas.")

This Challenge the Process behavior is about how leaders help others learn, which we've just acknowledged is essential for leaders themselves. Just as we suggested you help students become more aware of opportunities around them, here we expand the focus to how the leader enables others to innovate and take risks. This time the emphasis is not on developing and challenging one's own skills and abilities; it is about finding opportunities where other students can try new things, take some risks to experiment, and learn from new experiences.

This leadership behavior is about how leaders help bring others along. They do this in part by finding places where others can experiment and try new things. Student leaders can be fearful of taking risks that involve others and might prefer to do something themselves. However, the strength of the group comes from engaging all of its members.

Leaders create a place or environment where it's okay for people to take a chance and try a new idea, strategy, or approach. Yet young leaders can be hesitant to try something new, even though many young people have no problem challenging entire systems. This behavior, though, is about leaders helping others to try new things and take a chance on something that will benefit the group. And if whatever they try doesn't work out, leaders step up and look for the lessons that can be learned and help others see them as well. It is all too common for people to focus on the negative and what went wrong.

Talk with your students to see if they can identify opportunities they might have missed recently with their groups—times when they could have tried something new. Ask them to be specific about what those opportunities were so they can identify and take action the next time they arise. Challenge your students to identify their own insecurities and move beyond them so they can help others move beyond theirs. Talk about how this behavior shows up when leaders engage others in the group, and encourage them to take advantage of new prospects. When people try new ideas, be sure that their efforts are recognized and acknowledged, and successes (small wins) are celebrated. Enjoy the value in what the group members experienced and how the group got better.

Help your students think about this leadership behavior by asking these questions (also found in the *Student Workbook*):

1. Where can you go to get some new ideas or learn how to do something differently from the way you do it now?
2. Look at something you are doing now that is challenging for you or your group. Write down three actions different from what you are doing now that might address that challenge.
3. Look at something that your group is doing well or is well known for. Write down three actions, in addition to what you are doing now, that might improve on or even expand on this success.
4. How can you make it easy for others to try out new things and take a risk? How can you let them know that it is all right for them to experiment and teach them that from these trials, the group can gain greater understanding of what can be accomplished?

CHALLENGE
THE PROCESS

> "When things don't go as we expected, I ask, 'What can we learn from this experience?'" (Student LPI Report: "Asks, 'What can we learn?'")

Having a failed experience isn't pleasant for anyone. We all would rather succeed than fail. We all naturally have things that don't go as expected. However, learning from an experience that didn't work can show students the value that less successful outcomes provide.

Many young leaders haven't had much experience with failure in their groups or perhaps as a leader. They may in fact shy away from opportunities or situations where there is a high potential for failure. If they have struggled, they might simply move on to the next new thing, hoping to forget the experience as quickly as possible. Fear of failure can explain why some don't take risks, or certainly not huge risks. There can be a sense of embarrassment that comes from being judged by peers. Yet we know that leaders can learn a great deal from their failures if they take the time to explore and study these experiences. And in most cases with young leaders, a failure doesn't quite do the damage they think it does.

Help your students recognize that something valuable comes from every situation, including those in which they don't get everything right and when things don't go as expected. This could range from simple disappointment in the outcome to a wide spectrum of unsuccessful results. Ask your students to take note of an experience the next time something doesn't go as expected. Have them identify what they learned from the endeavor that they can incorporate the next time something similar happens. Encourage your students to think intentionally about the connection between what they learn from unsuccessful experiences and what they can apply to their next opportunity and how there would be little to no learning without mistakes.

Help your students think about this leadership behavior by asking these questions (also found in the *Student Workbook*):

1. What experience did you recently have that didn't go as you expected?
2. What are one to three specific things you learned from this experience that will benefit you in the future?
3. For each item you just identified, write how you can use what you learned when you have another opportunity to experiment.
4. Are there ways you have come to think about mistakes that have made you resilient? How can you share your own experiences with mistakes and learn from them with others you work with?

FURTHER ACTIONS TO IMPROVE IN CHALLENGE THE PROCESS

A list of suggested actions follows that you can tell student leaders to try out in order to improve in Challenge the Process. Some of the specific leadership behaviors in the Student LPI that are influenced by these actions are listed by number following each suggestion (see Appendix A for the complete list of Student LPI statements and behaviors).

1. Make a list of tasks that you perform that are related to your various leadership activities. For each task, ask yourself, "Why am I doing this? Why am I doing it this way? Can this task be eliminated or done significantly better?" Based on your responses, do you see where you can develop other skills? Identify those skills and look for applicable opportunities within your leadership activities where you can work to develop the skills you have identified. (3, 8)

2. Make a list of the things your group does that are basically done the same way as they have always been done before. For each routine, ask, "Are we doing this at our best?" If yes, then carry on! If no, look for ways to change to make it better. (8, 18, 28)

3. Continue to observe and learn about what makes other leaders successful, and then think about your own skills. Which skills do you see those leaders having that you don't have? Perhaps you believe you have those skills but need to strengthen them. Talk to those individuals and ask for their suggestions on what you could do to get stronger. If you don't have that opportunity, write down the skills or abilities you want to work on and ask an advisor, teacher, coach, or student life staff member to help you find places at your school or organization where you can develop those skills. (3, 13)

4. Ask others in your group what frustrates them about the organization. Make a commitment to change three of the most frequently mentioned items that are frustrating people and probably hindering the group's success. (13, 18)

5. Identify a process in your group that's not working, and take action to fix it. Learn from your experience. (18, 28)

6. Experiment by doing something you are not currently doing that will benefit your group—perhaps something new you can do within a project or event you are already working on. You might find something new you can do together that can meet a goal of your group. Make your experiments small, and learn from them for future larger experiments. (8, 28)

7. Eliminate "fire hosing" (throwing water on every new idea without giving it consideration). Remove from your group's vocabulary the "That'll never work" phrase or "The problem with that is . . ." At the very least, give new ideas the benefit of discussion and reflection. Recognize that even if the first idea isn't valuable, it might lead to others that are. (8, 18, 28)

8. Call or visit your counterparts in other organizations at your school, another school or group, or another community (both those in groups similar to yours and different from yours). Find out what they are doing and learn from their successes and challenges. Copy what they do well and use their failures as a guide for improvement. (13, 28)

9. Set achievable goals. Tell people what the key milestones are and review them frequently so that you and they can easily see progress. (23)

10. Eliminate the phrase, "That's the way we did it last year," from all discussions. Use the results of past programs or projects to learn from, but don't fall into the trap of doing something the same way simply because it's easier. (8, 23, 28)

ACTIVITIES TO LEARN ABOUT AND APPLY CHALLENGE THE PROCESS

Now that your students have been introduced to the ideas of Challenge the Process, here are some experiential activities that can be used to deepen their learning and guide them to experiment with the leadership behaviors.

Activity 5.1

We Need More Parking

Overview

This activity is a small group exercise that challenges students to look for alternative solutions to the work they do as leaders and help leaders practice the behaviors associated with

Challenge the Process. This activity provides the opportunity for students to practice the concept of outsight and helps them learn about searching outside their group or team for innovative ways to improve. In this activity, students learn about experimenting through idea generation and have the chance to think about how different ideas can influence various outcomes.

Objectives
Students will be able to:

- Understand and apply the concept of outsight to use with their groups to find innovative ways to improve
- Take the initiative in experimenting
- Learn the impact on change from asking, "What can we learn?"

Time Required
60 to 90 minutes

Materials and Equipment
1 envelope for each group
13 strips of paper (8 1/2 × 2 inches) for each envelope

Process
1. Organize students into small groups of five or six, with each group having the same number of students. Assign each group an identifying number (e.g., group 1, 2, 3). This activity is intended to address a challenge with campus parking. The issue of parking is a common problem for a number of reasons on many campuses. However, if your campus, school, or organization does not have this issue, substitute a school or organization issue that is of common concern with your constituency.

2. Describe a general or specific problem related to the parking issue on your campus (or other service or offering for your students). For example, students might complain it takes too long to find an open parking space on campus and the parking office responds by claiming there are plenty of spaces available based on the number of cars on campus at any given time. Or, parking permits are too expensive. Or, there are no convenient parking spaces; the faculty and staff get all of the good spots and students pay so much to park but have to walk fifteen minutes to get to class.

3. Once you describe the problem or issue to your students, explain that each group is a team charged with generating possible solutions to improve or resolve the situation. The groups should be challenged to identify ten strategies to address the issue that would be "reasonable" solutions. For example, if the amount of available parking is insufficient and a group poses a solution to "build more parking spaces" (which is obvious but involves many other aspects for that to happen), ask the group to go deeper with their idea.

This could be identifying a reasonably accessible location on campus for additional spaces that includes a suggested funding source for new construction; for example, adding more spaces may require an increase in the parking fee. Or the group might be able to identify an appropriate location that could provide one hundred temporary parking spaces with little construction expense. The groups will not understand all of the intricacies of their potential solutions, but your goal is simply to get them thinking more critically about their suggestions than the obvious.

Facilitator Cue

Challenge groups to think about the lowest common denominator. For each solution, present the action steps that would be needed to reach that solution from the point they are at now.

1. In this first round, allow thirty minutes for each group to identify their ten solutions, write them on the slips of paper, and place them in an envelope. Once time has expired or each group has finished, exchange envelopes among groups (the groups can pass their envelope to the group on their right). Be sure that the envelopes are numbered by the original group.

2. The next round requires each group to review the solutions they have been handed in the envelope from the other group. They briefly review the original group's ideas (emphasize that this is not an evaluation). If there is an idea that isn't clear to any group in this round, they may ask the originating group for more information or clarification. The assignment is for the groups to identify three additional (new) solutions to the original list of their neighboring group (hence the additional three strips of paper). Allow no more than twenty minutes for this segment.

3. Once this round is completed, have each group identify the top three potential solutions they see in the envelope they are holding (their neighboring group's envelope) and allow each group about three to five minutes to share their choices. The originating group can also provide insight to any solutions that they provided.

Facilitator Debriefing for Students

Lead a discussion for the last segment of this exercise on how your students experienced the challenge of identifying solutions for this issue that they experience every day as a member of their community. Use these processing questions to inspire the conversation:

Round 1: When you have been involved in other organizations and have faced a challenge or problem, roughly how many potential solutions did your group come up with before you did something? With this activity, what did it feel like to have to identify so many solutions to a problem? Why would you want to identify so many solutions?

Facilitator Cue

Typically student groups don't go through such an arduous process. By challenging them to continuously come up with possible solutions, you are helping to demonstrate ways to look for and think about opportunities and stretch beyond their group's narrow vision of thinking only about the obvious. Look for examples of outsight that groups might have used (and for groups that did not use outsight as much) and compare the differences in ideas).

Round 2: How did you address not having enough information to develop a solution? What was it like for you to create a solution for something that you face every day but have no responsibility for (or little understanding of what would be required to resolve the problem)?

Facilitator Cue

Help students think about the importance of taking a first step to getting started and how obstacles, real or self-imposed, can impede forward movement. Discuss how waiting until the conditions are right is not necessarily a productive strategy for leaders to help their groups work toward their shared vision.

Round 3: How does this experience relate to what you think leaders deal with on a regular basis—that is, what are the common characteristics of your experience that you think leaders also typically experience and must work to overcome?

Facilitator Cue

Consider how leaders deal with situations that many times they inherit—conditions they might not have any real responsibility for or control over and discerning them from conditions they can influence.

Additional Discussion

If you have time, the groups can collectively discuss what they think the best solution is and use that experience to evaluate their ability to think critically about how leaders face issues that are more complex than they seem at first. Many times the answers seem obvious (whether they are or not), yet extraordinary leadership is required to achieve the desired outcome.

Activity Variation

You may assign different issues to each of the original groups. If there are multiple organizational or school issues you would like your students to address as leaders, provide a scenario to each group, and follow the same instructions above. This technique requires groups in the second round to think about a new situation rather than simply to see if they can add some of their solutions to a problem others have addressed.

Activity 5.2

Take It One Step at a Time

Overview

This reflective exercise helps break large challenges into small actionable steps, generating small wins. It can also involve the use of outsight by including pairings or small group work.

Objectives

Students will be able to:

- Use core elements of Challenge the Process to generate clear, actionable next steps
- Experience the outsight provided by a peer who is unfamiliar with the challenge

Time Required

15 to 45 minutes

Materials and Equipment

Notebook paper
Flip chart and markers

Facilitator Cue

Explain that there will never be a shortage of challenges in our lives; it's how we approach those challenges that matters. Have students identify a challenge they face right now that feels so overwhelming that they can't seem to get started to face it, get past it, and move toward their goal. *Example:* "What big challenge are you facing in your life right now? Do you feel stuck in how you will meet this challenge? Does it feel too big to tackle?"

Process

1. Ask your students to create three sections on a blank tablet or piece of paper (or illustrate on a flip chart):
   1. Current Challenge
   2. Perceived Obstacles
   3. Small Step/Small Win Opportunity
2. Ask the students to describe the obstacle in the first section with as much detail as needed for someone else to understand the situation.

3. Ask them to list the obstacles they believe are in the way of making progress past that challenge.

4. *Self-reflection:* Ask your students to see if there is one small thing they believe they can do to make some progress even if it doesn't completely resolve the problem.

5. *Pairs or small groups:* Depending on the time available, have students pair up and share their example but not reveal their small step/small win ideas. Let the other person offer ideas from a fresh perspective. Then the first student can share his or ideas. Usually students end up with a clear next step and confidence they can tackle the issue. For groups of no more than four students, allow enough time for each person to get feedback from the others (about ten minutes per person) and use the same process.

Reflection and Connection to the Model

- Ask students at the end of the exercise if everyone came away from it with something they can do, however small, to move forward. Help your students see how the ability to break a challenge down into smaller steps made potential solutions or resolutions more accessible.

- Help your students see how the perspective of others (an example of outsight) provided new insight.

Activity 5.3

Movie Activity: *Apollo 13*

The Five Practices of Exemplary Leadership show up in many movies. This activity features selected clips that illustrate the use of Challenge the Process. Included is a brief synopsis of the film, a description of the clips that showcase the practice, followed by a series of questions for students to answer or consider.

Movies are a great way to spark creative thinking about how The Five Practices show up in real life. While the clips listed here are clear examples of Challenge the Process, look for examples of any of the other practices or leadership behaviors.

Movie

1995. Director: Ron Howard
Screenplay: William Broyles Jr. and Al Reinert
Distribution: Universal Pictures
Rated PG for language and emotional intensity

This movie is based on the book with the same title cowritten by Jeffrey Kluger and James Lovell Jr., one of the astronauts on the *Apollo* space flight to the moon in 1970. *Apollo 13* was the third U.S. space mission to put a man on the moon.

Synopsis

In the film, the spacecraft *Apollo 13* suffers a massive explosion while on its way to the moon in a section of the craft where the oxygen tanks are located that puts the lives of the three astronauts at risk: James A. Lovell Jr., the commander; John L. Swigert Jr., the command module pilot; and Fred W. Haise Jr., the lunar module pilot. For nearly six days, the ship and its crew are handicapped by the explosion and are without a plan to return to Earth safely. The NASA space program is still young and has never before encountered this situation.

Scene Descriptions

The following two scenes illustrate Challenge the Process. You can view these scenes as individual clips, stopping to discuss them in between, or as a collective sequence with discussion afterward. In each scene, you will find examples that you can use to supplement the conversation about leadership and Challenge the Process (as well as other leadership practices).

Theme: Failure Is Not an Option. Begins in chapter 32 on the DVD at approximately 1:19:42 (1 hour, 19 minutes, 42 seconds) to 1:21:07.

In this scene NASA realizes that the carbon monoxide levels in the astronauts' command module are becoming dangerously toxic. If the levels continue to rise, all three astronauts will die. Lowering the levels requires a special system to filter out the carbon monoxide, but the existing system is not working as designed because of the damage to the craft. The on-the-ground NASA chief urgently brings together some of his staff to identify and resolve the problem. The leader of that team brings an assortment of random parts and items that they know the astronauts can access on the spacecraft. The team must find a creative way to construct a functioning filter system in order to reduce the carbon monoxide levels and keep the astronauts alive. In essence, they must find a solution by successfully putting a square peg in a round hole.

Theme: More Power Needed. Begins at chapter 44 on the DVD at approximately 1:47:50 to 1:50:50.

One of the on-the-ground astronauts is working to develop a plan to provide the power the command module needs to reenter the Earth's atmosphere. The damage to the command module is significant: many of the batteries and power systems have been damaged. The crew needs most of the on-board systems fully functional so they can safely reenter the atmosphere and land. In this scene, pay attention to what the on-the-ground astronaut, Thomas Mattingly, does to determine a solution to the power problem.

Leadership Lessons from *Apollo 13*

Discussion Questions for "Failure Is Not an Option"

1. What did you see happening in the conversation with the NASA director before the team develops a solution?

2. What did Gene Krantz (the mission control flight director) do to help the team craft a solution?

3. How do you think Krantz's interaction made the team feel? How might that have affected their performance?

4. What are the team's first steps in working to find a solution?

Discussion Questions for "More Power Needed"

1. Although Mattingly was seemingly working on a solution alone in the capsule, he also had a team helping him. What did you see him doing that worked to define a solution with the help of his team members?

2. What examples did you notice of learning from mistakes?

Discussion Questions for Both Scenes

1. What risks were apparent in either of these situations, and how did the teams and individuals address them?

2. How might past experiences have influenced the work either group was doing?

CONNECT CHALLENGE THE PROCESS TO MODULE 8: PERSONAL LEADERSHIP JOURNAL

The Personal Leadership Journal is available to help students shape their ongoing learning about each practice. Depending on the time outside the classroom or formal workshop the students have available, this tool can be woven in as homework. There are three sections:

Section 1: Intended to be completed once students have had an opportunity to do a thorough review of their Student LPI report. We anticipate that some may choose to use this resource outside the classroom or formal workshop time, but it is valuable in or outside the class, and the facilitator is encouraged to use it in the environment that suits the needs of the student. For those not using the Student LPI, this section should be completed after students have a good understanding of Challenge the Process and the behaviors aligned with that practice.

Section 2: Intended to be completed after students have taken action. It will help guide them on their next targeted action step.

Section 3: Intended to support ongoing and independent exploration of Challenge the Process.

PRACTICE SUMMARY

As students learn to Challenge the Process, they will make mistakes, individually and as groups. These mistakes become opportunities if they allow them to be. Helping others view change as a positive part of their journey together is what leaders do. They also understand that embracing change and the challenges that go along with it is not easy. People need to believe in themselves and others; they need to feel both competent and confident to face the unknown that is inherent in challenging the status quo. That is where the next practice, Enable Others to Act, begins. In the next module, you will help students explore the leader's role in giving people what they need to make extraordinary things happen.

MODULE 6

Enable Others to Act

Practice Overview and Guided Discussion

PRACTICE SUMMARY

Leaders know that they cannot achieve great success alone. They know it take partners to make extraordinary things happen on teams, in small groups, or in larger organizations. Exemplary student leaders create an atmosphere of mutual respect and trust that allows people to rely on each other and work hard together. They build groups that feel connected and help people take ownership for the group's success.

Getting people to work together begins with establishing and then sustaining trust. It also requires a clear set of cooperative goals that are based on the values and the vision the group shares. Leaders understand how being trustworthy is the reciprocal of trusting others. They focus on "we," not "I."

Leaders realize that power is an expandable resource and strive to make each person feel empowered. They realize that empowering others is essentially the process of turning followers into leaders themselves. Great leaders, in other words, create more leaders.

Leaders understand that the process of strengthening others starts with the leader. They allow others to grow by letting them work on tasks that are critical to the success of the group and choose how they will take on their tasks. Leaders ensure that individual efforts are visible and recognized by others, and they facilitate the connection to others for support.

All of these behaviors make up Enable Others to Act. Leaders understand that when a group has a well-defined set of values and a compelling vision of what they would like to achieve, there are going to be challenges on the road to success. Facing challenges with an open mind and clearing the way to success by learning from mistakes and recognizing small wins are at the core of Challenge the Process. At the heart of Enable Others to Act is how the leader gives other people the confidence and competence to face the challenges they will certainly encounter.

FRAMING ENABLE OTHERS TO ACT FOR YOUR STUDENTS

Enable Others to Act builds on a basic truth that achieving great things happens not as the result of one person's efforts but from the combined efforts of many. This basic truth can be a stumbling block for young leaders who are driven to achieve, feel responsible for the outcome, and therefore decide to act alone. We hear them say, "I'm not sure I can trust some people in the group to do what they're responsible for. It's easier to just do it myself." We've

It wasn't my personal best. It was our personal best.
—SUSAN COHEN

all experienced that feeling from time to time, especially when under pressure. The practice of Enable Others to Act, however, assumes that leaders truly believe that working together brings greater achievements than working alone. They build relationships upon mutual trust and foster people's confidence and competence in working together effectively. The leader stays focused on the success of the group, not personal achievement.

Consider asking your students:

- When have you ever stepped in to cover for someone who failed to come through for the group? What impact did it have on you? What impact do you think it had on the group?
- How is it the leader's job to strengthen members of the group? If it is not the leader's job, whose job is it? If it is the leader's job, how does he or she do that?

Framing Commitment 7: Foster collaboration by building trust and facilitating relationships.

NOTE

Remind students that for each practice, the first commitment refers to their thinking as a leader, their frame of mind, and how they make decisions.

Leaders believe in the potential of others and let them know they do. They also do what it takes to help people achieve that potential, creating an atmosphere of support and trust.

Consider asking your students:

- Think of a time a leader believed in you when you might not have even believed in yourself. What impact did it have on you? How did it make you feel about that leader?

Our team was able to create a notion of trust amongst one another, so that in any given situation, we could trust the other to do the right thing.
—JORDAN GOFF

- Think of a time someone gave you something to do and then stepped in and did it himself or herself because that person didn't like how you were doing it. What impact did that have on you? How did that treatment make you feel about that leader?

Leaders demonstrate their trust in others before asking to be trusted by others. That means taking the risk of disclosing what they stand for, value, want, hope for, and are willing and unwilling to do. They also share their concerns about what it will take to succeed, engaging all the strengths in the group, and encouraging group ownership of success.

Consider asking your students:

- Think about a time someone said to you, "Will you trust me on this?" and you thought, "Why should I?" Think about a time someone asked, "Do you trust me?" and you knew your answer was, "Absolutely!" What was the difference between these two instances?
- Think back to your personal-best leadership experience. What did you do to get everyone involved? What did you say to get people engaged and committed to success?

Listening to what others have to say and appreciating their points of view demonstrates respect for them and their ideas. People listen more attentively to those who listen to them. By asking for the perspective of others and getting them to share information, leaders make certain that people feel involved in making decisions that affect them.

Consider asking your students:

- What do you notice happening in your group when the same people do most of the talking? What can you do to bring those who are quieter into the mix?
- Think of a time you spoke with someone who made you feel as though you were the most important person in the room. What did that feel like? What was it that the person did that made you feel the way you did?

No one can do it alone. For a positive experience together, people must have cooperative goals and roles. Each person's job should make a contribution to success, be meaningful to him or her, and be unique to the outcome.

In order to build collaboration, you need to let go of responsibility and give others a chance to take it on. By entrusting others with responsibility, you are letting them know you believe in them and that you have confidence that they can achieve it.
—ANA ABOITIZ

Leaders help establish trusting relationships within a group, so that people at all levels treat one another with fairness and respect. Leaders make sure they understand the interests of all members of the group or team and help them understand each other's interests and how each can gain more from collaboration than competition or independence.

Although many relationships won't last because of the changing environment, leaders treat every relationship as important to future success, and they encourage others to act in the same fashion. Human networks make things happen, and the best leaders are in the middle of them. Every leader needs to invest time and effort in building and nurturing a web of relationships.

Consider asking your students:

- What is your experience in being part of an organization that had an inner circle and an outer circle of members? What was the result of that dynamic?

- If you were the leader of that group, what could you have done to bring those circles together? What benefit might that have had? How might you begin connecting your circles today? Are there groups that share synergies that you might have never thought about connecting?

Framing Commitment 8: Strengthen others by increasing self-determination and developing competence.

Remind students that the second commitment refers to the actions leaders take.

> I began to spend most of my time helping others develop their leadership skills and taking on bigger projects. I found that the best way to lead was to inspire others and help them become competent leaders themselves.
> —REGAN BERGMARK

Creating a climate in which people are fully engaged and feel in control of their own lives is at the heart of strengthening others. As part of enabling others to act, student leaders do what it takes to build both confidence and competence in their fellow students so each will recognize and use their unique abilities to help the group succeed.

Leaders build confidence by listening to the ideas of others and acting on them, involving them in important decisions, and acknowledging and giving credit where credit is due. Leaders build commitment by giving employees latitude and autonomy. People can lead and feel that they are making a difference only when they get to exercise choices about key decisions being made and actions being taken.

Consider asking your students:

- What difference does it make to you if a job is assigned to you as opposed to being able to choose the job you will be responsible for on a large project?
- Think of someone in your group you could draw out by asking his or her opinion. How will you make sure that person knows you are sincere in asking?

Leaders build competence by organizing work to build up a person's skills and experience. They share power, engaging others in decision making and letting people determine their own path for completing tasks. This sharing of power demonstrates profound trust in and respect for others' abilities. It instills confidence and also builds competence, strengthening each member of the group and the group as a whole.

Consider asking your students:

- Think of a time when you were assigned a role you knew nothing about but had someone who was supportive and let you figure it out on your own. What happened? What was the result?

- What is your tendency to take charge and make assignments? If you tend to do that, is there another approach? What is your tendency to sit back and let others do the assigning? Is there a way to step up, ask for a new or challenging job, and let people know you are hoping to grow and learn from the experience and welcome their support?

HELPING STUDENTS UNDERSTAND AND APPLY THE BEHAVIORS OF ENABLE OTHERS TO ACT

The specific strategies and guiding questions around each of the leadership behaviors statements that make up The Five Practices of Exemplary Leadership can help you in developing your students as leaders. The statements listed are the same behaviors in the Student Leadership Practices Inventory. We recommend having your students complete the Student LPI, so that they can understand how frequently they already exhibit these behaviors and which of them they want most to focus on.

Use these ideas to help your students understand their leadership behavior and then apply it. You can work with your students to focus specifically on one area that they can work on to develop a greater frequency of the behavior. Focusing on all six of the behavior statements for Enable Others to Act helps students increase the frequency of their behavior for this practice.

NOTE For each behavior, you will find two iterations of the statement that describe the behavior: the statement as it appears in the Student LPI and how the behavior is described in the student report that is generated from taking the Student LPI.

Enable Others to Act Behavior Statements

> "I treat others with dignity and respect." (*Student LPI Report:* "Treats others with respect.")

One of the major issues that students are dealing with personally is their own sense of self. They are trying to reconcile who they are with who they think they need to be or should be. Naturally this involves how they view and treat others. Imagine a student who is trying to figure out her own values, what independence is for her, how she can succeed, what she is going to do in life, and so on. So much of her focus is on herself that she is still struggling to learn the true values that others can bring to the table.

The idea that respect must be earned puts the onus almost totally on the other person. Leaders realize that they can be more vulnerable and show others that there is a place for them to contribute and that they are valued members of the organization. This attitude toward others fosters a greater sense of trust in them. While one might not agree with the positions and ideas others hold, it is imperative that they are engaged and listened to and that they know their ideas and opinions are valued and respected. When leaders choose to appreciate others for what they offer and demonstrate confidence and trust in others' abilities, they are showing a great sense of dignity and respect for those in the group.

Help your students think about this leadership behavior by asking these questions (also found in the *Student Workbook*):

1. Describe the responsibility you think a leader has for respecting and valuing everyone in the group. How is that different from liking everyone in the group?

2. If you don't take the time and energy to get to know others in your group who are different from you, what impact would this have on the group? on the experience others have in the group?

3. Describe your general relationship with other members of your group. Are there any characteristics in your description that suggests you don't get along with or value others in the group? Without naming names, think about the people you don't find yourself really connecting with. Why is that? What could you do to strengthen that connection? Are there any common grounds on which you and these other individuals could begin to develop a relationship?

> "I actively listen to diverse points of view." (*Student LPI Report:* "Actively listens to diverse viewpoints.")

Listening is a skill that many people take for granted. The confusion between the interpretations of listening versus hearing can make it difficult for students to embrace this behavior. Can you imagine the scenario of a parent telling his or her young child to do something, over and over and over, each time getting the reply, "I heard you, Mom. I heard you, Dad" (said with an attitude, of course!). These responses naturally related to "hearing."

At the crux of this behavior is what we call active listening: being truly engaged in what the other person is saying and really hearing what the other person means. Only when leaders are actively listening can they be open to others' views in such a way that they will take them seriously. Giving lip-service to diverse points of view won't work because it simply means, "I'll let you say what you have to say, but I don't really care or see the value in it." Of course, the risk in listening to others is that one might change his or her opinion, which is precisely what leaders are always open to considering.

Students are exposed to many opportunities to practice active listening and can work to understand that they don't have to accept or agree with everything everyone says. Still, actively listening to others' points of view provides access to endless ideas, solutions, information, and creativity that might be easily disregarded when not paying attention to others and by carrying the attitude of simply trying to move on to the next item.

Help your students think about this leadership behavior by asking these questions (also found in the *Student Workbook*):

1. How do you react to others' points of view when you don't agree with them? How do those reactions affect your ability to lead and affect your relationships in and with the group?

2. Define what active listening means to you. Then describe a time when you really listened and responded in some way to what another person had to offer. Describe another experience when you felt you weren't really interested in listening to what someone else in the group had to say. What were the different impacts on the interactions or relationship between you and the other person, and what was the subsequent impact on the group?

3. What are three things you think you can do to better listen to and understand another person's view that differs from yours? What might you gain from that point of view that would help you be a better leader?

> "I provide opportunities for others to take on leadership responsibilities." (*Student LPI Report*: "Provides leadership opportunities for others.")

This leadership behavior, as we are sure you can imagine, requires the leader to let go. If the leader is providing opportunities for others to lead, that means he or she is not trying to do everything alone. So much of the spirit and intention with the leadership practice of Enable Others to Act is about helping others build competence and confidence. This leadership behavior statement embodies the spirit of that responsibility, when the leader recognizes the need to find opportunities for those in the group to develop those two characteristics, among many others.

Young leaders can get caught up in a lot of "me." They take on too much or take over when someone doesn't do his or her part. Recognizing that others in the group could be well suited for any number of assignments or tasks is a wise way for leaders to work with those with limited experience. Then they work on helping newer members take these experiences and build them into opportunities to be ready for more advanced leadership roles. As others get more experience and develop a greater sense of confidence and competence, then they are great candidates to fill in and take the ball and run with it when someone else might be a "no show." These two common scenarios are ripe times for leaders to identify ways to help develop others as leaders in their group. Younger leaders can be anxious about this behavior for the reasons mentioned, yet they can be shown how bringing others along as leaders is not a threat to them but another way for them to strengthen their own leadership capacity. When leaders do this, they move from focusing on "me" to "we" (or from self to others).

Help your students think about this leadership behavior by asking these questions (also found in the *Student Workbook*):

1. Identify opportunities in your group for others (without any concern for official titles or leadership positions) to take on leadership responsibility. Name five opportunities. Then expand the list to ten. What can you do to help others take advantage of these opportunities?

2. What responsibility do you think a leader has in helping others in the group grow and develop as leaders? At what point do you think you can help someone do that? Do you instead say to yourself, "He can't be a leader," or, "She has to figure that out on her own"?

3. How would your role or day-to-day responsibilities or work as a leader change if others in the group took on more leadership? What opportunities would this provide for you? What advantages do others taking on more leadership give the group?

ENABLE
OTHERS TO
ACT

> "I give others a great deal of freedom and choice in deciding how to do their work."
> (*Student LPI Report:* "Gives people choice about how to do their work.")

This leadership behavior represents some of the same challenges we find in how leaders work to support others' decisions. It requires at the onset the capacity to trust those in the group. As with providing an environment where others' decisions are respected, providing freedom for others to do what they are responsible for, and even more beyond that, is a critical aspect of effective leadership.

In essence, this is about the leader bringing others along as leaders. The best way to do that is to get out of the way and let others have the autonomy to do what they are tasked with. Again, it is sometimes difficult for students to let go. They may find it much easier to say, "I can just do it myself. It will be faster, better, and, well, it will be done right." We think that leaders who respond this way are not really saying they want something done right but that they want it done their way.

No group will ever reach its potential if the leader tries to do all of the work. Nor will the group succeed if the leader delegates the work to others and then micromanages everything. Leaders recognize that they can't do it alone. To be the best that they can be, and that the group can be, requires the talents of others. It has been said that leadership is lonely at the top. If your students feel this way about leadership, this is a clear sign that they are not allowing others to do what they are capable of doing in the way they see fit. When others are brought along, they gain confidence, skills, and strengths, and they are moving themselves up there to be with the leader.

This leadership behavior has much embedded in it about the importance of leadership. For younger leaders, it can be a very big challenge to address. They are constantly faced with the idea of failure (whether they just assume this possibility to be true or hear it from elsewhere). If they let others do the work and it's not done right, the group will fail. Young leaders get the message that they must always be the one to step in and take over. If the group fails, they think, "I have failed because I am the leader." But just as a leader cannot take all the credit for the success of a group, the leader is not solely responsible for its failures. Therefore, it is imperative to always tap into the talents of others for a group to function successfully.

Facilitator Cue

Consider leading a discussion about the idea of failure and what positive influences and results can come from such an experience. Younger leaders may feel a sense of shame, inadequacy, or hurt pride if the desired outcomes in their tasks and projects are not realized. They may believe they can avoid failure if they simply do everything themselves, but this does not promote Enable Others to Act, help others develop competence, or build confidence or trust.

Help your students think about this leadership behavior by asking these questions (also found in the *Student Workbook*):

1. To what degree would you say you allow others to do their work as they see fit? To what degree do you feel you can let go completely and let others in the group take full responsibility for what they are doing? Describe the feelings you have when you do or don't do this.

2. What are some specific things you can do to help members of the group develop a greater sense of confidence in the work that they do? If you did these things with each person in the group, what do you think would happen to (1) the individual and (2) the group?

3. If you are more likely to try to take on and do many things for the group yourself, think for a moment why that is. Write a reflection about (1) when and why you take on responsibilities or tasks that others in the group could do and (2) what you are most concerned about or afraid of if you don't assume those responsibilities but provide them for others to assume.

4. What does success or failure mean for you and your group in the context of giving other people more freedom and choice in deciding how their work will be accomplished? Considering the situations you are reflecting about, if they didn't result in what you expect, what is the worst outcome that could happen? How will that affect you, the others in the group, and the group as a whole?

"I foster cooperative rather than competitive relationships among people I work with." (*Student LPI Report*: "Fosters cooperative relationships.")

It is widely understood that younger students are going through several developmental stages, one of which is how they develop relationships. Many students are increasingly being challenged by or already working to find the balance between autonomy and independence, a relatively new concept to them, and establishing relationships with others that are much different from the dependent types of relationships with family, teachers, and others that they have been accustomed to. In other words, leadership development is about being able to understand how to be independent contrasted with the understanding that as a leader, you can't it do it alone.

For student leaders, the question is how they can establish their own identity and demonstrate competence while at the same time realizing that they need to have cooperative and giving relationships with others. They may think, "I need to be better than everyone else," which can manifest easily as a competitive sense. Yet in becoming leaders, and people of and with influence, students need to recognize that they must work to develop relationships with others in order to embody the characteristics and true meaning of leadership. As they develop more mature relationships, they have a greater focus on characteristics such as honesty, commitment, compassion, openness, and curiosity, all of which serve leaders well.

This leadership behavior tells us that we need to work to challenge young leaders on how they intentionally look at the relationships they have with those they lead and sincerely work to understand the importance of cooperation for the good of the group and the group's purpose instead of continuing to prize the competitiveness that favors the individual.

Help your students think about this leadership behavior by asking these questions (also found in the *Student Workbook*):

1. On a scale of 1 to 10, with 1 being low, how would you rate your sense of competitiveness? To what degree do you think competition should play into being a leader, specifically as it relates to working with others in the group? Without letting go of or altering your sense of being competitive, describe how cooperation would differ in working with others when a leader takes on this characteristic more.

2. When you find yourself being competitive with others in your group, what are the conversations, sharing of ideas, debates, and decisions like? How would they be any different if a more cooperative environment were present?

3. What can you do as a leader to create a cooperative environment within your group? How would you describe the balance you think is necessary between cooperation and competitiveness? Is this any different when you are looking within the organization and its members or when you are looking at the greater purpose of the organization as it relates to other groups?

4. What circumstances, characteristics, or conditions do you think need to be present for a group to have a more cooperative environment? As a leader, what could you do to help create that environment?

"I support the decisions that other people make on their own." (*Student LPI Report:* "Supports decisions other people make.")

It can be very difficult for younger leaders to let go of anything for which they have developed a sense of ownership. Part of the letting go requires that they trust and value the decisions others make. Leaders need to recognize that there can be many ways to accomplish something and that they do not have the final word.

Having the confidence in one's self to know that people in the organization are generally looking out for the organization's best interests and then allowing them to have the autonomy to make decisions about areas for which they have responsibility, or where they can make a positive impact on the group, goes a long way in building relationships, trust, and confidence in others. Will those others make some poor decisions? Most likely. But would that possibility be any different if the leader kept full control and power over all the work of the group and made a poor decision? Most likely not. Leaders must recognize that they don't have all of the necessary knowledge, skills, awareness, or information. Therefore, they must first allow others the autonomy to make decisions and then support those decisions.

Leadership is about creating an environment where others can flourish. Someone who doesn't value the experiences of those in the group or doesn't honestly accept that others have the ability to make wise and thoughtful decisions is simply managing people to follow whatever he or she says. This approach never has the same impact as leadership.

We have talked of the need for leaders to support others' decisions. What exactly does that mean? Is it that the leader simply agrees with the decision, no questions asked? Of course not. Debate and discussion are almost always necessary with any decision of substance. Still, leaders who have worked to develop trust and confidence among members of the group will create an environment in which everyone is respectful and encouraging of others' ideas so that it is safe to debate.

Help your students think about this leadership behavior by asking these questions (also found in the *Student Workbook*):

1. As a leader, what are your beliefs about letting others make decisions independently? How much latitude do you give them to make decisions? What kinds of decisions do you let them make? What tolerance for risk (the degree to which you think something will go wrong) do you have for others making decisions?

2. Look at how your behaviors affect other individuals. If you let others make decisions and support them in what they decide and give them freedom to follow through, how does that affect them as individuals? If you are more restrictive much of the time, how do you think that affects others as individuals? Be as specific as possible.

3. If you responded generally favorably that you let others make decisions, support them in what they decide and give them freedom, what is the impact on the group? If you are more restrictive in most ways, how do you think that affects the group? Be as specific as you can be.

FURTHER ACTIONS TO IMPROVE IN ENABLE OTHERS TO ACT

A list of suggested actions follows that student leaders can try out in order to improve in Enable Others to Act. These are also found in the Student Workbook. Some of the specific leadership behaviors in the Student LPI that are influenced by these actions are listed by number following each suggestion (Appendix A provides the complete list of Student LPI statements and behaviors).

1. Teach others in your group to become leaders. Leaders bring others along to be leaders. Take some specific steps, perhaps starting with just one or two people, to help them develop their leadership abilities. (24, 29)

2. Make a point of encouraging others to take on important tasks or projects. Put the names forward of people in the group you believe would be well suited for a certain project. Similarly, talk with them about taking on a responsibility on behalf of the group, letting them know that you have confidence in their ability and judgment. (4, 14, 19, 24, 29)

3. Take another approach to item 2 by asking someone else to lead a group meeting or do a presentation so he or she can gain that experience (or any other experiences you identify). Then coach along the way to assist and support that person in this new capacity. (4, 14, 24, 29)

4. Give something up altogether that you do on a regular basis. Don't just give up something you don't want to do, but find someone in the group you think would grow from taking over this task as a regular responsibility. Be sure to let him or her know that you are not just getting rid of something you no longer care to do or think is critical; rather, explain how this represents an opportunity for this person to grow and develop. (4, 9, 19, 24, 29)

5. Identify someone at your school or in your community who is known as an exceptional leader. Contact that person and find out if you can follow or shadow him or her for a few hours to learn about how you can become better working with others. (4, 9, 14)

6. Improve relationships and develop a greater sense of trust with group members by doing something together outside regular group activities. Find ways to interact informally so you and they can build stronger bonds with each other. (4, 9, 14)

7. For the next two weeks, see how often you can replace "I" with "we" as you lead a group. Work to develop the philosophy and understanding that leadership is about the group or the team, not one individual. Every time you think about saying "I'm going to . . . ," say instead, "We can do this . . . " (4, 9, 14, 29)

8. Ask an athletic coach if you can watch a practice or team meeting to see how he or she helps athletes develop new skills or identify and reach new goals. Think about how you can apply these lessons to the groups to which you belong. (4, 9)

ACTIVITIES TO LEARN ABOUT AND APPLY ENABLE OTHERS TO ACT

Now that your students have been introduced to the core ideas of Enable Others to Act, here are several experiential activities that you can use to deepen their learning and allow them to experiment with the practice.

Activity 6.1

What Makes You Trust Someone?*

Overview

This activity helps students examine the role of trust in effective leadership by evaluating their own level of trust in leaders they have known.

Objectives

Students will be able to:

- Understand the importance of trust in effectively leading others
- Understand the potential impact on relationships within an organization or group
- Identify behaviors that promote trust

Time Required

20 to 30 minutes (facilitators can manage the length of the discussion time allowed)

Materials

Flip chart and markers
One Trust Worksheet (Figure 6.1) per participant (included in the *Student Workbook*)
Writing materials (paper and pencil or pen)

Room Setup

Students should be seated in groups of four or five. If you have a larger number, account for the additional discussion time to hear from each member.

Process

1. Have students turn to the Trust Worksheet in their workbook. Have each student identify two people in leadership positions or roles: one they trust and one they do not trust. (They do not have to be from a current situation.)

---

*This activity was adapted from "What Makes You Trust Someone?" submitted by Sherri Dosher for J. M. Kouzes, B. Z. Posner, and E. Biech, *The Leadership Challenge Activities Book* (San Francisco: Jossey-Bass/ Pfeiffer, 2010).

2. Instruct students to complete their worksheet individually. Under the "Trust" column, have them list the traits or behaviors that lead them to trust that person. Under the "Lack of Trust" column, have them list the traits or behaviors that prevent them from trusting that person. Then have them list the impact this person's behavior had on them and their work. (Allow about five minutes for this.)

3. Once they have completed the worksheets, have students discuss their results with others in their small group. Allow about two or three minutes for each student to contribute.

4. Ask the students to identify common themes and record those on a flip chart to share with the larger group. Looking at the collective themes from the flip charts, ask students how these themes relate to commitment 7 from Enable Others to Act: Foster collaboration by building trust and facilitating relationships.

5. Summarize with questions like these:
   * What does this tell us about how important trust is to effective leadership?
   * What happens when there is a lack of trust?
   * What is the impact when trust exists?
   * What behaviors will you focus on to establish trust?

Figure 6.1 Trust Worksheet

Trust	Lack of Trust
List the traits or behaviors you believe helped you trust this person.	List the traits or behaviors you believe led you to not trust this person.
What impact did this person's behavior have on you and your work?	What impact did this person's behavior have on you and your work?

Activity 6.2

Blindfolded Square

Overview

This activity works best with groups of ten to eighteen students. It is often used in connection with Inspire a Shared Vision but is also effective for exploring the second commitment of Enable Others to Act: Strengthen others by increasing self-determination and developing competence. In this context, it helps demonstrate how enabling (or disabling) others contributes to (or takes away from) the group's ability to reach their common goal.

Objectives

Students will:

- Understand the importance of sharing information when leading others
- Experience the importance of listening to others
- Identify behaviors that help others feel (or not feel) confident and capable
- Experience behaviors that contribute to (or hinder) high levels of group performance when faced with a new problem in unusual circumstances

Time Required

30 to 45 minutes

Materials

One rope approximately 100 feet long and one blindfold per participant. For smaller groups of eight to twelve, the rope can be shortened to 50 to 70 feet. The ends of the rope should be securely tied together.

Room Setup

You will need a room large enough to accommodate the number of students you have to spread out into a circle with the length of rope you are using.

Facilitator Cue

Safety note: Clear the space of any obstacles that could cause falls (e.g., chairs, tables, wastebaskets). Watch closely during the untangling phase that elbows and faces do not get bumped. If you are outdoors, keep people from walking on uneven surfaces, and watch for tree roots, holes, and other obstacles.

Process

Part 1: Setting Up the Activity

1. Have the students arrange themselves in a circle with the facilitator in the middle. Do not let them see the rope.
2. Ask them to blindfold themselves.
3. After everyone is blindfolded, stand in the middle of the circle with the rope coiled in your hands.
4. Have students place both hands out, palms up, so the rope can be placed in their hands. One by one, place a section of the rope in each student's hands.

Part 2: Instructions

1. The objective is to form a large, perfect square with the rope using its entire length. Each side of the square must be equal to one-fourth of the rope's length. When the group has reached consensus that they have formed the square, they lay the rope on the ground, remove their blindfolds, and inspect the results.

Facilitator Cue

The goal of the exercise is to produce a square: four equal sides with right angles. Typically groups assume they have done this but then find that the result doesn't meet either requirement: the sides are different of lengths, and the angles are not 90 degrees.

---

2. In achieving the objective, the group must adhere to the following guidelines:
   a. Blindfolds may not be removed at any time (unless a person is getting distressed; see option 5b).
   b. You must keep both hands on the rope and not let go.
   c. You may hold only one section of the rope.
   d. You may slide along the rope or let it slide through your hands as necessary to accomplish the objective.
3. The group has fifteen minutes to accomplish this objective.
4. As the facilitator, you may answer questions, but do not reveal any other information.
5. Options
   a. During the process, quietly remove one person's blindfold. Don't say anything about why you have done so. Typically it takes a while for the student to realize he or she is now empowered to give clear direction but hesitates to say or do anything. In the debriefing, it is interesting to explore why the person reacted in this way. What assumptions did he or she make that kept him or her from taking the lead with the information he or she now had?

b. If you have too many students or if someone is unable or unwilling to be blind-folded, you can assign him or her the role of observer. Have this person take notes on how the experience unfolds: Who took charge? Who helped make significant progress in the exercise? What did people say? Were their comments positive or negative? How did that affect the group?

Part 3: Debriefing

Facilitator Cue

Help guide the conversation back to the commitments of Enable Others to Act. Emphasize the role of trust (or lack of trust), the importance of sharing information and letting people say how they worked together, and what it was that they needed to feel competent and confident.

- Have students answer these questions in their *Student Workbook:*
  1. What did you notice about who took charge? Who helped make significant progress in the exercise? What kinds of comments did people make? Were they positive or negative? How did that affect the group?
  2. What feelings did you experience during the activity?
  3. Where did those feelings come from?
  4. What group or individual behaviors contributed to your feelings?
  5. What specific behaviors helped the group reach their objective?
  6. What specific behaviors got in the way of the group reaching its objective?
  7. Do you ever see yourself doing these behaviors (either type)?
  8. What lessons can you take away from this activity to reduce frustration or confusion and raise your group's performance level?

Facilitator Cue

If you had an observer, start the debriefing by having that person relay what he or she saw. If this person attaches meaning to any action (e.g., "She got frustrated when he said that"), be sure to ask, "What made you say she was frustrated?" and validate it with the student in question: "Were you frustrated?"

Activity 6.3

Movie Activity: *Freedom Writers*

The Five Practices of Exemplary Leadership show up in many movies. This activity features selected clips that illustrate the use of Enable Others to Act. Included is a brief synopsis of the film, a description of the clips that showcase the practice, and then a series of questions for students to answer or consider.

Movies are a great way to spark creative thinking about how The Five Practices show up in real life. While the clips listed here are clear examples of Enable Others to Act, look for examples of any of the other practices or leadership behaviors.

Movie
2007. Director: Richard LaGravenese
Screenplay: Richard LaGravenese
Distribution: Paramount Pictures
Rated PG-13 for violent content, some thematic material and language (no scenes for this activity include those elements)

Synopsis
This movie is based on the diaries written by students at Woodrow Wilson High School in Los Angeles. Teacher Erin Gruwell is in her first teaching job and works with at-risk students challenged by a community of violence, drugs, gangs, and little hope or promise to achieve anything beyond the life they know.

Scene Descriptions
The descriptions of two scenes in the film illustrate Enable Others to Act. You can view these scenes as individual clips, stopping to discuss them in between, or as a collective sequence with discussion afterward. In each scene, you will find examples that you can use to supplement the conversation about leadership and Enable Others to Act (as well as other practices).

Theme: Heroes. Begins in chapter 12 on the DVD at approximately 1:21:03 to 1:28:55
> This scene depicts an example of how relationships evolve and trust is built as people get closer to each other, in this case by finding experiences they can share. The students' inspiration comes from each other: after reading *The Diary of Anne Frank*, they believe that they can bring Meip Gies (the woman who helped hide Anne Frank from the Nazis in World War II) to speak at their school. They find within each other that they have the capacity to make this seemingly impossible visit happen. As they gain confidence in themselves, they develop a stronger belief that anything is possible if they are creative and persistent.

Theme: Courage. Begins in chapter 13 on the DVD at approximately 1:28:57 to 1:34:18.

Facilitator Cue

You can continue into this scene from the "Heroes" scene, though we suggest you pause before "Courage" begins to discuss the unique things that happen in "Heroes."

This scene begins with two characters struggling to resolve difficult personal situations: Marcus, who has been estranged from his mother for years, and Eva, who, in the finale to one of the film's substories, must testify in a murder trial involving a man from a street gang that her father (who is currently in jail) belongs to. Eva is being pressured because of her father's gang affiliation to testify that someone other than the accused actually committed the murder. Her honest testimony puts her and her family in danger of retaliation.

Leadership Lessons from *Freedom Writers*

Discussion Questions for "Heroes"

1. Describe the examples of Enable Others to Act you saw in "Heroes."
2. In the latter part of the scene, when Ms. Gies is speaking, how do her words show Enable Others to Act?

Discussion Question for "Courage"

1. What Enable Others to Act behaviors did you observe in "Courage"?

Discussion Question for Both Scenes

1. In either scene, what other practices or leadership behaviors did you notice?

CONNECT ENABLE OTHERS TO ACT TO MODULE 8: PERSONAL LEADERSHIP JOURNAL

The Personal Leadership Journal is available to help students shape their ongoing learning about each practice. Depending on the time available outside the classroom or formal workshops students have available, this tool can be woven in as homework. There are three sections:

Section 1: Intended to be completed once students have had an opportunity to do a thorough review of their Student LPI report. We anticipated that this module would be used outside the classroom or formal workshop time, but this is not required. For those not using the Student LPI, this section should be completed after students have a good understanding of Enable Others to Act and the behaviors aligned with that practice.

Section 2: Intended to be completed after students have taken action. It will help guide them on their next targeted action step.

Section 3: Intended to support ongoing and independent exploration of Enable Others to Act.

PRACTICE SUMMARY

Leaders use their authority and power in service to others because they believe in them and know how well capable and confident people perform. People neither perform at their best nor stick around for very long if they are made to feel weak, dependent, or alienated. When a leader helps group members feel strong and capable, they often do more than they ever thought possible. Authentic leadership is founded on trust, and the more people trust their leader (and each other), the more they take risks, make changes, and keep organizations and movements alive. Through that relationship, a leader enables others to act as leaders themselves.

We have explored how credibility serves as the foundation of The Five Practices of Exemplary Leadership through Model the Way and how leaders align the actions they take with the values they hold to maintain that credibility. This source of shared values produces visions of how things could be better; this is the heart of Inspire a Shared Vision. A compelling vision of the future provides a beacon for the group that grounds its members as they face the challenges inherent in change.

Challenge the Process is about thinking openly and intentionally about how things could be thought of or done in a new and different way and how to help everyone feel safe to take risks, experiment, and learn from the mistakes that are bound to happen. Enable Others to Act focuses on giving people the confidence and competence they need to do things differently than they have in the past and move forward despite their doubts. But if we refer back to our definition of leadership—the art of mobilizing others to want to *struggle* for shared aspirations—it is clear that the journey is not an easy one. That is where Encourage the Heart comes in. In the next module, we examine another essential leadership practice and explore the power of touching the human heart.

MODULE 7

Encourage the Heart

Practice Overview and Guided Discussion

PRACTICE SUMMARY

Making extraordinary things happen in organizations is hard work. The climb to the summit is arduous and steep. Leaders encourage others to continue the quest. They expect the best of people and create self-fulfilling prophecies about how ordinary people can achieve extraordinary actions and results. By maintaining a positive outlook and providing motivating feedback, leaders stimulate, focus, and rekindle people's energies and drive. These are all essentials to Encourage the Heart.

Leaders have high expectations of both themselves and their constituents. They provide others with clear direction, substantial encouragement, personal attention, and meaningful feedback. They make people feel like winners, and winners like to continue raising the stakes!

Leaders give heart by visibly recognizing people's contributions to the common vision. They express pride in the accomplishments of their groups. They make others feel like heroes by telling the rest of the organization about what these individuals and the group have accomplished.

Celebrating group accomplishments adds fun to hard work and reinforces group spirit. Celebrations increase people's network of connections and promote information sharing. Fostering high-quality interpersonal relationships enhances productivity along with both physical and psychological health.

Leaders help organizations establish a clear set of shared values and a compelling vision of the future based on those values. When they do, they are demonstrating the first two practices—Model the Way and Inspire a Shared Vision—which drives them forward into the unknown. Facing that unknown requires them to Challenge the Process and provide people with the confidence and competence they need to face their quest—Enable Others to Act. But the road to success is not an easy one. If achieving the extraordinary is a marathon, then Encourage the Heart provides the water stops along the way. With it, people have an essential ingredient for sustaining their struggle; without it, they won't go the distance. Encourage the Heart may be the last of The Five Practices of Exemplary Leadership, but it is by no means the least important.

FRAMING ENCOURAGE THE HEART FOR YOUR STUDENTS

Exemplary leaders understand that all people need to feel valued, feel they are part of something, and have a clear sense of purpose. They strive to provide that for the group and start by always being on the lookout for what people do that supports the values and the vision of the group and helps move everyone closer to their shared goal. They make it their job to catch others in

When I gave praise on people's work, they seemed to work harder because they were proud of the work that they had done.

—SHERI LEE

the act of doing things right and then recognize them in a meaningful and genuine way, providing the sense of value and purpose the individual needs. Leaders also strive to recognize people publicly, reinforcing the vision and values of the group and creating a sense of community.

Consider asking your students:

- In what ways do you need to be recognized to perform at your best?
- If you are recognized for your efforts in a way that feels genuine, what is the impact on your performance?

Framing Commitment 9: Recognize contributions by showing appreciation for individual excellence.

NOTE

Remind students that for each practice, the first commitment refers to their thinking as a leader, their frame of mind, and how they make decisions.

There are few needs more basic for anyone than to be noticed, recognized, and appreciated for his or her efforts. Leaders pay attention to and notice what people are doing right and the contributions they are making, no matter how small, that support the group. Next, they recognize the contribution, acknowledging its impact on the group and the journey to success.

Consider asking your students:

- Think of a time you were recognized for something you did that you thought nobody noticed. How did that feel? What did it make you feel about the leader who recognized your effort?
- What did that leader do or say that made a difference to you?

Leaders personalize recognition, finding the acknowledgment and reward that is special and unique for each individual and the accomplishment. Spontaneous, unexpected rewards—such as a sincere word of thanks demonstrating a clear understanding of the contribution, public praise, or a small meaningful gift—often have more impact than a big, formal reward. The words used or gift chosen should have some special meaning to the recipient and be tied to what you are thanking him or her for. In other words, it shouldn't be a generic "thanks for showing up" sort of token but a thoughtful expression of the leader's gratitude and understanding of the person. Such things demonstrate that the leader cares and is genuinely interested in seeing everyone succeed.

Showing that you care about someone is a simple yet overlooked quality to the success of a leader.

—DAVID BRAVERMAN

Consider asking your students:

- Can you share an example of being recognized that felt genuine to you? What made it feel that way?
- What is the most meaningful way to recognize someone in a group?

Framing Commitment 10: Celebrate the values and victories by creating a spirit of community.

> **NOTE** Remind students that the second commitment refers to the actions leaders take.

If you notice what people are doing that is good and supports the cause, that's great, but it's not enough. At the other end of the spectrum from individual, personalized recognition are celebrations—significant occasions when respect and gratitude are proclaimed publicly. Celebrations renew a group's sense of community and recall the values and history that bind them together. The best leaders know that every gathering of a group is a chance to renew commitment and strengthen the sense of community (the "common unity"). These events offer opportunities to communicate and reinforce the actions and behaviors that are important to realizing shared values and goals. Celebrations also provide social support. In strengthening community, student leaders create a sense of belonging and team spirit, building and maintaining a foundation of social support that is especially crucial in stressful times.

By publicly praising people, you make a statement for how you wish other people, not directly involved in the praise, to work and act. Public, well-deserved, and fact-based appreciation can hence have a multiplier effect.

—KAJSA RYTTBERG

Consider asking your students:

- What makes you feel part of a group or organization? Can you identify the context in which those feelings came about?
- How might you create that feeling for your group or organization?

Leaders take advantage of the way public celebrations remind people that we're all in this together and depend on one another. They reinforce the fact that it takes a group of people working together with a common purpose in an atmosphere of trust and collaboration to make extraordinary things happen. Celebrating together reinforces the fact that extraordinary performance is the result of many people's efforts. Celebration and community, however, have a significant impact only when they're genuine. Elaborate productions that lack sincerity are more entertainment than encouragement. By celebrating people's accomplishments visibly and in group settings, leaders don't separate individuals from the group, but instead create community and sustain team spirit by honoring what has been accomplished to move the group forward. By making celebrations genuine and basing them on consistency with key values and attainment of critical milestones, leaders reinforce and sustain people's focus and spirit; they encourage the heart.

Consider asking your students:

- Think of a celebration you've attended that you felt honored the group as well as individuals. How would you describe what that was like?
- What are the key ingredients in a celebration that made it feel genuine? What are some things that may be less important or not necessary at all?

Facilitator Cue

Listen for the things that make the celebration genuine, not just generic.

I found that encouraging my teammates was one of the easiest and most beneficial things I could do to make the team better.
—KRISTEN CORNELL

HELPING STUDENTS UNDERSTAND AND APPLY THE BEHAVIORS OF ENCOURAGE THE HEART

The specific strategies and guiding questions around each of the leadership behavior statements that make up The Five Practices can help you in developing your students as leaders. The statements listed are the same leadership behaviors that are in the Student Leadership Practices Inventory. We recommend having your students complete the Student LPI, so that they can understand how frequently they already exhibit these behaviors and which of them they want most to focus on.

Use these ideas to help your students understand their leadership behavior and then apply it. You can work with your students to focus specifically on one area that they can work on to develop a greater frequency of their leadership behavior. Focusing on all six of the behavior statements for Encourage the Heart helps students increase the frequency of their behavior for this practice.

NOTE

For each behavior, you will find two iterations of the statement that describe the behavior: the statement as it appears in the Student LPI and how the behavior is described in the student report that is generated from taking the Student LPI.

Encourage the Heart Behavior Statements

> "I encourage others as they work on activities and programs." (*Student LPI Report:* "Encourages others.")

A good place to begin with this leadership behavior statement is to think about the word *encourage*. What might that mean to students? Is it something like cheering for someone? Or could it be a note or card when someone is feeling down? Could it be a simple "attaboy" or "attagirl"? We think of encouraging others as a way to make them "want to" keep going. In our definition of leadership, we talk about "mobilizing others *to want to.*" By that, we are saying that to get others to want to, leaders need to encourage them often. Notice that the behavior statement says "as they work on." This means encouraging others while they are working on things for the group, not just afterward. We wrote earlier of the water that is needed to keep going in a marathon race. Leaders need these times of encouragement to keep going, to help their followers "to want to."

Help your students think about this leadership behavior by asking these questions (also found in the *Student Workbook*):

1. What are some of the ways you have encouraged others as they were doing something? What reactions did you get from those people? Describe how that encouragement made a difference in the person, group, or outcome of the project—or all of these.

2. What are some simple ways you can acknowledge someone while he or she is in the middle of a project or assignment? What would you need to be looking for in order to recognize someone and then how would you use what you have learned? Are there some experiences that you can learn from where you might have missed opportunities to recognize others?

3. How do you think group members could be even more committed to the group than they already are? What are some things that you think would help some in the group to be more committed but others not as much?

> "I express appreciation for the contributions people make." (*Student LPI Report:* "Expresses appreciation for people's contributions.")

First, look at this leadership behavior statement from the perspective of support. What do we mean by that? Does it mean money, people resources, things the group needs? Is it simply encouragement? In fact, it might be all of those things. It's important for leaders to provide the group with the tools they need to do their work because it reinforces that they believe in the group members and care about what they are doing. Support demonstrates to people that what they are doing is valued and important. This essential message to constituents becomes even stronger when leaders expect the best from them. If a leader were to expect just average efforts, then group members wouldn't feel compelled to give any more than the minimum necessary, which can create a climate of mediocrity. However, when a leader expects the best, equips a group with what they need to perform at the highest level, and stands up for those in the group, people will feel supported and encouraged.

Leaders can also show support by their example here. A leader who is willing to do what the group members are doing will be trusted. In this way, he or she develops an understanding about what others are experiencing. This trust and understanding is another form of support.

The second part of this leadership behavior statement is simply recognizing excellence as group members demonstrate it. Both behaviors, providing support and expressing appreciation, go hand in hand. If a leader expects the best but then doesn't show appreciation, it won't take long for the group members to begin performing at or below average. Through appreciation, leaders show that they care about and support their groups. Leaders need to talk to and listen to their group members to learn what is important to them in order to support them. This is not particularly difficult to do, though it does require leaders to make an intentional effort to listen and understand.

Help your students think about this leadership behavior by asking these questions (also found in the *Student Workbook*):

1. How can you show appreciation to your group members for the various kinds of work that they do? Can you think of some of the more common ways to show appreciation to the group? Do you know specifically what expressing appreciation for their contributions means to those in the group? In other words, what expressions of appreciation do people in the group need that you can provide?

2. Share a few ways in which you have been showing appreciation to individual members in the group. If you can recall only a few instances of this, what can you specifically do to notice more individuals and what they are doing, and what can you do to take a moment to thank them?

3. Sometimes when groups are working on big projects, there can be a great sense of pressure or stress. These can be tremendous opportunities for you to learn what group members need. How could you take advantage of these opportunities to watch for and listen to what the members could use to help them carry on? What role would you see yourself in during these high-pressure times in terms of supporting others?

ENCOURAGE
THE HEART

> "I make sure that people are creatively recognized for their contributions." (*Student LPI Report:* "Creatively recognizes people's contributions.")

Whereas the previous leadership behavior statement is about supporting and showing appreciation for people's contributions, this one is about knowing the individuals in your group and recognizing them in a way that has meaning to them. Leaders know that personal recognition is eloquent, and the recipient is likely to remember it for a long time to come. When leaders take the time to know the people in their groups, they can more easily be creative in finding a way to meaningfully recognize each individual.

While this leadership behavior focuses on how leaders recognize an individual, it becomes part of how they celebrate the accomplishments by bringing the group together. In exhibiting this behavior, leaders would not give everyone a generic certificate. Instead they recognize each person in a way that is directly related to what that person did and in a way that matters to him or her individually. Could that be done with a certificate? Yes, as long as there was some meaning behind that certificate. For example, when the leader hands out a certificate while telling a story about what the individual did and what it meant to the organization, the meaning behind the certificate becomes clear. Could this be done with some other token or gift? Yes, of course. What is given as a token is simply a physical symbol of the message, and while the token can carry meaning, it carries only as much meaning as the genuineness of the appreciation to the person being recognized.

Help your students think about this leadership behavior by asking these questions (also found in the *Student Workbook*):

1. Begin to keep a list or journal of various ways in which you could recognize someone. While this practice focuses on how the recognition needs to be personal to the individual being acknowledged, it can be helpful to have a tool like a journal or log in your smart phone to trigger some ideas for yourself when the time comes.

2. To make recognition personal, you need to know the people in the group. The majority of organizations that you are involved in won't be so large that you can't get to know everyone to some degree. Challenge yourself to reach out to those in the organization you might not know so well and get to know them better. In fact, identify three people in one of the groups you're in, and make a commitment to get to know him or her more personally over the next few days. Leaders who know their groups well will also be more aware of the things members are doing so they can be recognized.

3. An easy way to keep track of what is important to people in a group is to keep a log of some sort. Just as you have a system for remembering phone numbers, birthdays, and e-mail addresses, you can keep notes, say in your smart phone, of things you want to remember about people—for example, favorite foods, sports teams, preferred colors, and music.

ENCOURAGE
THE HEART

"I praise people for a job well done." (*Student LPI Report:* "Praises people.")

Leaders understand that people perform at their best when they are acknowledged and recognized. This is something that needs to occur often and at times when those in the group do work that moves the group forward and makes the group better. Leaders who understand this leadership behavior and exhibit it often are able to do so because they are always on the lookout for people doing great work. In part, leaders need to be clear about what a job well done looks like. They present clear expectations based on the goals and the values of the group, and these expectations become the standards for the group. Leaders who are clear about expectations make it easier for those in the group to know what it means to do a job that helps the group improve. Nothing in this leadership behavior suggests that recognition needs to be held until a particular special event. While end-of-the-year banquets, for example, are common in schools, we don't want students to use only those occasions to recognize others. Help your students think about how they can be watchful for opportunities to praise those in their groups.

Help your students think about this leadership behavior by asking these questions (also found in the *Student Workbook*):

1. Name a time you were recognized for something you did. How did that feel? If you were to recognize someone else, would he or she feel the same way?

2. What do you think recognizing other people does for them? Why would praising someone for a job well done motivate, encourage, and engage that person? How does recognizing someone bear on his or her work and interactions in the group?

3. Think of someone you have seen in the past week do something meaningful for a group you are in. Did you do anything to recognize that person? Why or why not? If not, how might you still recognize that person now?

4. Make a list of twenty-five ways you could recognize someone for a contribution he or she might make. Don't consider what the recognition is or how practical it is. Just create the list. (We'll explore this again in another leadership behavior.)

ENCOURAGE
THE HEART

> "I make it a point to publicly recognize people who show commitment to shared values." (*Student LPI Report:* "Publicly recognizes alignment with values.")

The idea that leaders make a point of recognizing others implies a strong intention on the leader's part. Leaders who value their followers accept that recognition is important and that they must make it their regular routine to seek out ways to acknowledge others. In this particular behavior statement, we emphasize three things. First is the intent: making a point to do something. Next is that we understand that recognition has a much greater impact when it is public. It is important that this is done in an appropriate manner, which means, for example, that it doesn't embarrass the recipient. Still, there is a higher impact when others know what someone has done to better the group. The fact that recognition is public demonstrates that it isn't happening just because it's something nice to do for someone. Leaders know that recognition rises to a higher level when others can share in the celebration of what someone has done or accomplished.

Third is that leaders reinforce the group's values whenever they recognize someone for doing something that shows commitment to those values. Not only does this make the recipient proud and heartened knowing that others recognize his or her commitment to the group; it also sends a message to the rest of the group that there is great importance in their values. The values are not just some statements produced for the sake of creating them. Any group that understands and acknowledges those who commit to and perform around those values knows that they have a greater purpose.

Help your students think about this leadership behavior by asking these questions (also found in the *Student Workbook*):

1. As a leader, think about how the group's values look when they are being demonstrated or acted on. In other words, what is someone doing when he or she is demonstrating integrity (or whatever other values the group holds)? By reflecting on this, you know what to look for when people are demonstrating their commitment to the group's values.

2. Once you know what aligning one's behavior with the group's values looks like, the next step is to recognize that. Think about the when, what, and why of the ways you can do that. Think about how you can recognize someone for something he or she did. When did that person do it? What specifically did he or she do? And why does it matter to the group? Think these questions through and be prepared when the times arise for you to recognize others.

3. There are many ways to recognize someone publicly. One thing to consider is how comfortable various individuals in the group are with different types of public recognition. Think about some of the ways you could recognize someone publicly so you have a good collection of ideas to match an appropriate method with people in the group.

ENCOURAGE
THE HEART

> "I find ways for us to celebrate accomplishments." (*Student LPI Report:* "Celebrates accomplishments.")

Nearly everyone loves celebrations. Unfortunately when it comes to student leaders and groups, the tendency is to take only end-of-term or end-of-the-school-year opportunities to truly celebrate the accomplishments of the group or individuals in the group. If you recall again the water-for-the-marathon metaphor for Encourage the Heart, you know that marathon runners do not drink water only at the end of the race; they need it throughout the race. The same holds true for celebrating accomplishments. People perform better and with greater engagement if they are encouraged along the way. Organizations can feel that they are making a greater difference if they can celebrate their accomplishments as they go rather than trying to force everything into a year-end banquet where nothing is really being celebrated except the fact that they made it to the end of the year. Imagine if leaders were able to capture the enthusiasm and excitement of accomplishments, small and large, as they happened throughout the year. Leaders understand that bringing people together more frequently means involving them in each other's lives.

Leaders find times to celebrate small milestones along the way, a breakthrough on some major obstacle, or a goal that has just been met. They intentionally work to have the group celebrate what they have been working hard to accomplish. That way, relationships flourish, and trust is nourished. We know that celebrations build community and when you go beyond simply the professional, people will come to know and care about each other more.

The celebrations we are talking about don't have to be elaborate or even planned. They don't have to be big or expensive. They just have to be—and occur frequently.

Help your students think about this leadership behavior by asking these questions (also found in the *Student Workbook*):

1. Think about all kinds of ways that you could celebrate accomplishments of the group. Remember that this behavior focuses on "us," as in "the group as a whole." Describe five ways that you can publicly recognize the entire group for something they contributed. Try to think of ways beyond the traditional recognition dinners, social hours, or regular group meetings.

2. Think about how you can make various recognitions for the group in a public manner. There might be an occasion to recognize a committee within the group or the group as a whole. How can you let others know about the group's accomplishments in a way that recognizes the contribution the group makes, say, to the campus, school, or organization as a whole?

FURTHER ACTIONS TO IMPROVE IN ENCOURAGE THE HEART

A list of suggested actions follows that you can tell student leaders to try out in order to improve in Encourage the Heart. These are also found in the Student Workbook. Some of the specific leadership behaviors in the Student LPI that are influenced by these actions are listed by number following each suggestion (Appendix A provides the complete list of Student LPI statements and behaviors).

1. If your group is working on a larger project or event, identify small milestones along the way that would be appropriate places for you to celebrate. Don't wait until the

entire project is finished. Celebrating your success and progress along the way will encourage others to keep going. (10, 25)

2. As often as you can, share a story publicly with the group or other appropriate audiences about someone in the group who did something exceptional; that is, that person went above and beyond the call of duty. (5, 10, 15, 20, 30)

3. When recognizing someone, think of the "three Ws": who, what, and why. Recognize the person by name (*who*). Describe *what* the person did. You don't need to go into immense detail, but share enough of the story so others can see how exceptional the work was. Finally, tell *why* what the person did mattered to the group. Connect this person's work to the values of the organization to demonstrate that you recognize how he or she is truly making a difference to make the group better. (5, 20, 30)

4. Use informal times and gatherings to find out what others are doing that exemplify what the group stands for. Take a moment to recognize these people on the spot. (10, 20, 30)

5. When you talk with someone in the group and get to know him or her, find out what encourages this person. Ask how he or she likes to be recognized and what has meaning for him or her. You might ask about times in the past when something special was done for that person and what that meant. When the time comes, you will be prepared to recognize this person in a meaningful way. (5, 10, 15, 30)

6. Write at least three thank-you notes every week to those who are doing work (taking actions) that supports and improves the group. (5, 15, 30)

7. If you receive or hear acknowledgments of good work from others about people in your group, be sure to pass those comments along to them in a public way. You might read the note aloud at a meeting, put it on your group's website, or release it through social media. (5, 20, 25, 30)

8. Be on the lookout for creative gifts you can use to recognize and reward people. You can find inexpensive things in retail stores that you can easily relate a story to. You can also use things you might come across, such as photos, buttons, small stuffed animals, painted rocks, ribbons, or some other trinkets. It is not the gift but the thought and the story that goes with the gift that matter the most. (5, 10, 15, 30)

9. Create some tools anyone in the group can use to recognize others at any time. Preprint some note cards or pads, for example, or come up with a unique award or something that you can turn into a tradition for the group when others want to acknowledge exceptional work. (25, 30)

10. If you do have end-of-term or end-of-school-year activities, go beyond the typical certificate or plaque and be sure to put personal stories behind the recognition. If someone has been doing extraordinary work and really made an impact on the group, acknowledge those contributions by sharing them with the audience. You give greater meaning to the contributions by sharing a personal story about the individual. (5, 15, 20, 25, 30)

ACTIVITIES TO LEARN ABOUT AND APPLY ENCOURAGE THE HEART

Now that your students have been introduced to the core ideas of Encourage the Heart, here are several experiential activities that you can use to deepen their learning and allow them to experiment with the practice.

Activity 7.1

Web of Appreciation

Overview
This activity helps students acknowledge each other and creates a visual metaphor for the connection and unity of the group.

Objectives
Students will be able to:

- Acknowledge each member of the group for a specific contribution and identify how it contributed
- Build a physical web of yarn that represents the interconnectedness of the group
- Acknowledge that the more people rely on each other, the tighter and stronger the web becomes

Time Required
Allow 1 minute per person when estimating the length of the activity.

Materials
1 ball of string, or strong yarn. Using variegated colored yarn makes a beautiful web.

Room Setup
Students should be able to form a large circle without being too close together (1 foot or more between each person).

Process
1. Have students form a circle. Stand in the middle with the ball of yarn and explain the directions: each will unwind several yards of the string or yarn, hold it tight at that point, and then toss the ball to someone else.
2. Facilitator holds the end of the string or yarn and tosses the ball to the first person.

3. This person will then toss the ball to someone else in the circle he or she wants to acknowledge. Before tossing the ball, he or she identifies who the person is and says what that person did that warrants acknowledgment and why it mattered to the person holding the yarn and the rest of the group.

4. The person then gently tosses the ball. The receiving person repeats the process until everyone has a connection point with the yarn.

Facilitator Cue

You will create the visual metaphor for the group once everyone is holding onto the string or yarn. Ask them to hold it firmly and step back to tighten the web. Gently push against it to show how much stronger it is when everyone is involved and relying on each other. If one person drops the piece of yarn he or she is holding, show how it weakens the web. You can let the web drop or toss it in the air at the end in celebration of the group.

Activity 7.2

Recognition Cards

Overview

This activity offers the opportunity for anyone to easily and quickly recognize and show appreciation to someone right on the spot.

Objectives

Students will be able to:

- Develop the ability to regularly look for ways in which others exemplify the organization's standards
- Experience giving recognition as they see someone doing something that improves the group or shows commitment to the group's values—or both

Time Required

Varies per recognition. Students will use this resource to recognize others immediately as they see them doing something.

Materials

Box of business-size recognition cards (see Figure 7.1)

Room Setup

None

Figure 7.1 Sample Recognition Card

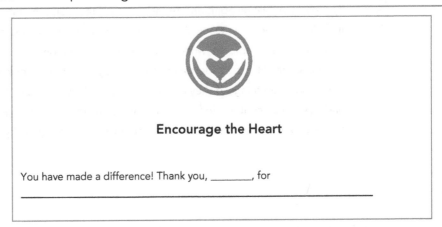

Encourage the Heart

You have made a difference! Thank you, _____, for

_____

Process

1. Provide every group member with a supply of the Encourage the Heart recognition cards.

2. Direct students to fill out the cards and use them whenever they see a group member (or any other student, for that matter) doing something that they believe exemplifies the standards of the organization, demonstrates the values of the organization, works to go above and beyond typical actions, provides a great idea, supports another member or helps them in some way become successful, or something else.

3. In one meeting each month (or at some other predetermined interval), you can ask students to share the cards they have given or received so the group can see the exceptional work that all members do that might go unnoticed in a typical day.

NOTE

While the recognition cards are an easy and convenient way to share encouragement among members, the group might not always be aware of how people are recognizing each other. It is important to make the recognition public by sharing some of the cards that were given out over a period of time.

Variation

If you are working with a group of student leaders or a student organization that has some physical space of its own, you can use a variation of this exercise as a recognition poster.

In this variation, use blank newsprint that you place on the walls around the office space. Cut the paper to a size (such as a half-sheet of typical newsprint paper) so that every member of the group has an individual page. Each member adds his or her name to it and can decorate the top of the paper as he or she chooses. Group members then can write encouraging notes on it to fellow members throughout the month. Each month, put up new sheets so the members can create their own journal of Encourage the Heart comments.

NOTE

The poster variation is a great way to celebrate the community of the group and easily provide public recognition. An inclination is that some members will be dejected if their peers don't write on their posters for all to see. This is a great opportunity to encourage people to write something reflecting on the specific behaviors of Encourage the Heart. Leaders and others always need to be looking for when people are doing good things. If they are working toward awareness of others' contributions and how those contributions demonstrate commitment to the group's values, it will be easy to have more than enough comments to add to any active member's poster.

Activity 7.3

Movie Activity: *Harry Potter and the Sorcerer's Stone*

The Five Practices of Exemplary Leadership show up in many movies. This activity features a selected clip that illustrates the use of Encourage the Heart. Included is a brief synopsis of the film, a description of the clip that showcases this practice, and then a series of questions for students to answer or consider.

Movies are a great ways to spark creative thinking about how The Five Practices show up in real life. While the clips listed here are clear examples of Encourage the Heart, look for examples of any of the other practices or leadership behaviors.

Movie

2002. Director: Chris Columbus

Screenplay: Steve Kloves

Distribution: Warner Bros. Pictures

Rated PG for some intense moments and mild language (the scene for this activity does not include those elements)

This movie is based on a book written by J. K. Rowling about a boy who attends a school for wizardry. Harry Potter spends his first year of school challenged with fighting for good and against evil.

Synopsis

Harry Potter, a first-year student at Hogwarts School of Witchcraft and Wizardry, is a member of one of four residential houses at Hogwarts that typically are in competition with each other in a number of sports and academic contexts. Harry makes close friends with many of the students, and his family history of wizardry makes him popular throughout the school. Still, some in the school despise him and create difficult and dangerous situations for Harry and his friends to face throughout the film. They all survive their first year relatively unscathed.

Scene Description

The following scene offers examples that you can use to supplement the conversation about leadership and Encourage the Heart (as well as other practices).

Theme: House Cup Winner. Begins in chapter 33 of the DVD at approximately 2:17:44 (2 hours, 17 minutes, 44 seconds) to 2:21:35.

Professor Albus Dumbledore, the headmaster of Hogwarts, is winding down the school year and awarding the house cup to one of four residential houses based on a series of competitive events and other contributions to the school. In announcing the winner of the year's house cup, the professor describes a number of actions that members of one house took throughout the movie.

Leadership Lessons from *Harry Potter and the Sorcerer's Stone*
Discussion Questions for "House Cup Winner"

1. What examples of Encourage the Heart did you see in this scene?
2. What things did the headmaster say in his remarks that makes this an example of Encourage the Heart? Is there anything he might have done differently?
3. Was there anything different about how the headmaster recognized each person?
4. After the remarks, did you notice anything happening with everyone in the banquet hall?

CONNECT ENCOURAGE THE HEART TO MODULE 8: PERSONAL LEADERSHIP JOURNAL

The Personal Leadership Journal is available to help students shape their ongoing learning about each practice. Depending on the time outside the classroom or formal workshop that students have available, this tool can be woven in as homework. There are three sections:

Section 1: Intended to be completed once students have had an opportunity to do a thorough review of their Student LPI report. We anticipated that this module would be used outside the classroom or formal workshop time, but this is not required. For those not using the Student LPI, this section should be completed after students have a good understanding of Encourage the Heart and the behaviors aligned with that practice.

Section 2: Intended to be completed after students have taken action. It will help guide them on their next targeted action step.

Section 3: Intended to support ongoing and independent exploration of Encourage the Heart.

PRACTICE SUMMARY

Leaders recognize and reward the actions and efforts of individuals that align with the group's values and contribute to its success. And they express their appreciation frequently, not limiting themselves to formal recognition. Leaders enjoy being spontaneous and creative in saying thank-you, whether by sending personalized notes, handing out carefully chosen prizes, singing songs, listening without interrupting, or trying any of myriad other forms of recognition. Leaders personalize recognition by knowing what's appropriate both individually and culturally and taking some time to think about what would be most meaningful to the person being recognized.

Leaders celebrate together to reinforce the fact that exemplary performance is the result of the efforts of many people. By celebrating accomplishments visibly and in a group setting, leaders sustain individual and group spirit and create community. Basing celebration on consistency with shared values and vision and critical milestones reinforces and sustains people's energy and focus. It helps them go the distance.

We have now examined each of The Five Practices of Exemplary Leadership. Once you have covered this material, there are many ways to help students do the deliberate practice required to be an exemplary leader. In the next module, we help you explore the opportunities for using the Personal Leadership Journal as a tool for self-exploration and ongoing leadership improvement.

MODULE 8

Personal Leadership Journal

OVERVIEW AND GUIDELINES FOR CONTINUING YOUR LEADERSHIP DEVELOPMENT JOURNEY

The last module in the Student Workbook is the Personal Leadership Journal, which students can use to plan and reinforce their continuing development as leaders. The journal is designed for students to use for independent work after participating in a leadership workshop or class. If your students are in an ongoing leadership program or you have a continuing coaching or advisory relationship with them, their journal reflections might be used in individual or small group conversations on their progress in meeting their leadership development goals.

The text of the journal is reprinted here.

•••

Your leadership development begins when you answer the call to accept personal responsibility to develop the leader within you. But it doesn't end there. The Leadership Challenge research tells us that this will be an ongoing process, one that requires deliberate and reiterative practice. That practice is most effective when you take some time to reflect on what you've learned along the way. That continued learning, beyond a workshop or a class, plays a key role in your ability to liberate the leader within. This Personal Leadership Journal is intended to support your ongoing leadership journey.

Each section of the journal is linked to one of The Five Practices of Exemplary Leadership and builds on your Student LPI feedback. Each is organized into three parts: (1) Take Action (a guide for committing to action), (2) Look Within (questions for reflection and further thinking), and (3) Ongoing Learning (ideas for refining the lessons from experience).

Take Action (What Do You Intend to Do?)

There is no substitute for learning by doing. The Student LPI data indicate that the more frequently you can demonstrate these essential leadership behaviors, the greater the possibility is that you will lead others to achieve extraordinary results. It is in the doing that you discover your potential to engage others in meaningful change. Use the journal to define the actions you will take.

Changing your behavior in any way can be a challenge, and taking small steps is one of the best ways to meet the challenge. For example, a soccer player who decides she wants to improve her game might take time to focus on one skill. Perhaps one day's practice is on building speed and another day on agility with the ball. Practicing the individual parts gives the player an immediate goal that aligns with the long-range goal of being a stronger player. The same applies here: find ways to demonstrate and practice the behaviors that will strengthen your leadership capacity. Every goal for tomorrow requires some action today.

A good way to identify those small steps is by committing to S.M.A.R.T. actions. This acronym stands for: **S**pecific, **M**easurable, **A**ttainable, **R**ealistic, **T**imely. Identifying S.M.A.R.T. actions can greatly increase the likelihood that you will keep your commitment.

Look Within (What Did You Learn from Taking Action?)

As you practice, take some time to reflect on what you are learning. Lessons are always available if you take the time to look within and listen. Get in the habit of taking a few moments of quiet time each day to answer the questions here. Note what you learn about yourself and from others. Find ways to apply that in the days ahead.

Ongoing Learning (What Will You Do Next Based on This Experience?)

In the practice modules in this workbook, we offered you some suggestions for actions to take to work on each leadership practice. The "Ongoing Learning" sections throughout this Personal Leadership Journal ask you to choose one of these suggestions and commit to it as a way to deepen your practice of the behaviors and refine your philosophy of leadership.

AFTER REVIEWING YOUR STUDENT LPI DATA

Facilitator Cue

The assumption is that your students will have completed one of the Student LPI products.

Take Action (What Do You Intend to Do?)

1. The leadership practices or behaviors I will focus on are:
2. Areas in my life where I will look for opportunities to take action:

Look Within (What Did You Learn from Taking Action?)

One way to build your commitment to leadership is to imagine the legacy you might leave down the road. Take time to reflect on and answer this question based on your current thinking.

1. I want to be known as a person who:
2. I want to be remembered as a leader who:

Ongoing Leadership Learning (What Will You Do Next Based on This Experience?)

1. Review your Student LPI report and note which practice you do the most frequently. What opportunities do you see to continue demonstrating that practice in the next week or two?

2. Review the thirty leadership behaviors that make up your Student LPI report, and note any that you want to understand more fully. What questions do you have about them?

AFTER REVIEWING THE LEADERSHIP PRACTICE OF MODEL THE WAY

Take Action (What Do You Intend to Do?)

Use your Student LPI report and what you have learned about Model the Way to take action based on one of the six leadership behaviors associated with this practice.

The leadership behavior I've chosen:

Your Actions

1. To demonstrate this behavior, the actions I need to take are:

2. Detail how each element of a S.M.A.R.T. action is addressed in your action plan.

   Specific: Is your action clear and simple? Does it answer the following questions?

   What do you want to accomplish?

   Who is involved?

   When will it take place?

   Where will it take place?

   Measurable: Is there a clear way to measure completion or success?

   Attainable/Action-Oriented: Can this goal be accomplished? How?

   Relevant/Reasonable: Is this action relevant for the goal you have in mind as a leader? How?

   Timely: Is a time frame attached? If so, what is it?

Look Within (What Did You Learn from Taking Action?)

1. What happened when you took this action?

2. What were the results of taking this action?

3. What did you learn about the value of demonstrating this leadership behavior?

4. What parts of this action were comfortable and easy? What was difficult? What might your answers tell you about yourself as a leader?

Ongoing Learning (What Will You Do Next Based on This Experience?)

Refine your philosophy of leadership: With deeper understanding of Model the Way, is there anything you would like to add or revise in your answer to the question, "I want to be known as a leader who_____"?

Commit to deepening your practice: The following are examples of things you can do to Model the Way that were suggested in Module 3. Review them, pick one from the list to commit to, or identify another way to practice Model the Way, and then describe what you will do to meet that commitment.

1. At the beginning of each day, reflect on what you want to achieve for that day. Think in terms of what you know is important to you and what in your schedule contributes to that importance. You might ask yourself, "How do I want to show up as a leader today?" At the end of the day, reflect on what happened. What did you do as a leader that you are most proud of? Where were the opportunities that you missed that you could take advantage of another day? Can you do anything tomorrow about those opportunities? What other actions can you take tomorrow to enable you to lead better? (1, 26)

2. If you are in any sort of group and have a formal, defined leadership role, see how you can work directly with or shadow someone else on the team. In essence, trade places with that person and work on something together. Use this as an opportunity to get feedback from others as to what you are doing related to their work in the group. (6, 16)

3. Use a planner, smart phone, journal, note app, or some other resource you use regularly to write notes to yourself about the commitments and promises you are making to yourself and others. Write the dates you have committed to fulfilling them, and check regularly on your progress. (1, 11, 26)

4. Focus on the little things that your groups or the people you lead are doing. You can become easily engaged in the larger projects or tasks, but remember that it is the smaller details together that help others (and the projects) achieve success. Without micromanaging, look for places where you can make a difference. Think about how you use the smaller things that need attention to reinforce what you and the organization stand for. (1, 6, 16, 21, 26)

5. Keep track of how you spend your time. What is important to you and what you value often shows up in how you spend your time and prioritize what you do every day and over the course of weeks and months. Look to see if you are investing large amounts of your time in things that are not that important to you or that you really don't value. The same might also be said about people and relationships. What can you do to adjust your schedule so that you are aligning your actions more with your values? (1, 6, 11, 21, 26)

6. If you are in an organized student group, visit other teams or groups at your school that are similar and even different from yours that you know to be considered strong groups.

Talk to their leaders, and ask about what they are doing that could give you greater insight into leading. You don't have to be talking about doing the same things to learn and get feedback from how others lead and work. Learn what makes the other group so great. (16, 21, 26)

7.   Study other leaders and organizations that you think live out their ideas and values as a group. These could be groups that you identified in action 6, or groups, organizations, or companies that are known to have strong values and demonstrate those values in their daily work. (1, 2, 16, 21)

Ways that I will practice Model the Way and how I will do that:

AFTER REVIEWING THE LEADERSHIP PRACTICE OF INSPIRE A SHARED VISION

Take Action (What Do You Intend to Do?)

Use your Student LPI report and what you have learned about Inspire a Shared Vision to take action based on one of the six leadership behaviors associated with this Practice.

The leadership behavior I've chosen:

Your Actions

1.   To demonstrate this behavior from Inspire a Shared Vision, the actions I need to take are:

2.   Detail how each element of a S.M.A.R.T. action is addressed in your action plan.
    Specific: Is your action clear and simple? Does it answer the following questions?
        What do you want to accomplish?
        Who is involved?
        When will it take place?
        Where will it take place?
    Measurable: Is there a clear way to measure completion or success?
    Attainable/Action-Oriented: Can this goal be accomplished? How?
    Relevant/Reasonable: Is this action relevant for the goal you have in mind as a leader? How?
    Timely: Is a time frame attached? If so, what is it?

Look Within (What Did You Learn from Taking Action?)

1.   What happened when you took this action?
2.   What were the results of taking this action?

3. What did you learn about the value of demonstrating this behavior?

4. What parts of this action were comfortable and easy? What was difficult? What might your answers tell you about yourself as a leader?

Ongoing Learning (What Will You Do Next Based on This Experience?)

Refine your philosophy of leadership. With deeper understanding of Inspire a Shared Vision, is there anything you would like to add or revise in your answer to the question, "I want to be known as a leader who_____"?

Commit to deepening your practice. Following are examples of things you can do to Inspire a Shared Vision that were suggested in module 4. Review them, pick one from the list to commit to, or define another way to practice Inspire a Shared Vision, and then describe what you will do to meet that commitment.

1. Talk with an advisor, coach, or staff member or teacher about how you might think of some new ways in which you can help a group look at its vision more clearly and about different ways in which the group might better align with its vision. (2, 12, 22, 27)

2. Take stock of what you get excited about with your group. How does that excitement influence what you can do to connect with others in the group? What conversations will help others see the possibilities you can explore together to better realize your vision? (7, 12, 22, 27)

3. Imagine that it's one year from today: What is different about the group? What has it accomplished? How is the group better off than it was a year ago? Why? (2, 7, 12)

4. Talk with individuals in your group about their hopes and aspirations for the organization. Figure out what is shared and how those things relate to what you personally envision for the group. Think about how the group's vision is or is not in alignment with what others in the group think. (7, 12, 17)

5. The next several times you meet or talk with people in your group gatherings, listen for the language they use. Is it tentative or noncommittal, such as, "We'll try," or, "We could/should"? Can you make sure that it is more positive and committed, such as, "We will!"? (7, 22, 27)

6. As a leader, ask yourself, "Am I in this role because of something I can or want to accomplish for myself?" or, "Am I here to do something for others?" Are you working to lead the group toward the group's shared vision or your own agenda? (12, 17, 27)

7. Sharing a vision requires clarity and confidence. If it is difficult for you to talk emphatically and confidently to a group, look for multiple opportunities, such as other student groups that involve public speaking, to speak in front of people no matter what the purpose. The more often you do this, the more confident and comfortable you will be in speaking situations. (22, 27)

8. Who are other leaders you find inspiring? Read about them to see how they communicate their vision for those they lead. What is it about what and how they say things that stand out to you and cause the reason for your inspiration? Think about how you can learn from what they say and do. (2, 12, 22, 27)

Ways that I will practice Inspire a Shared Vision and how I will do that:

AFTER REVIEWING THE LEADERSHIP PRACTICE OF CHALLENGE THE PROCESS

Take Action (What Do You Intend to Do?)

Use your Student LPI report and what you have learned about Challenge the Process to take action based on one of the six leadership behaviors associated with this practice.
The leadership behavior I've chosen:

Your Actions

1. To demonstrate this behavior from Challenge the Process, the actions I need to take are:

2. Detail how each element of a S.M.A.R.T. action is addressed in your action plan.
   Specific: Is your action clear and simple? Does it answer the following questions?
   > What do you want to accomplish?
   > Who is involved?
   > When will it take place?
   > Where will it take place?

   Measurable: Is there a clear way to measure completion or success?
   Attainable/Action-Oriented: Can this goal be accomplished? How?
   Relevant/Reasonable: Is this action relevant for the goal you have in mind as a leader? How?
   Timely: Is a time frame attached? If so, what is it?

Look Within (What Did You Learn from Taking Action?)

1. What happened when you took this action?
2. What were the results of taking this action?
3. What did you learn about the value of demonstrating this behavior?
4. What parts of this action were comfortable and easy? What was difficult? What might your answers tell you about yourself as a leader?

Ongoing Learning (What Will You Do Next Based on This Experience?)

Refine your philosophy of leadership. With deeper understanding of Challenge the Process, is there anything you would like to add or revise in your answer to the question "I want to be known as a leader who_____"?

Commit to deepening your practice. Following are examples of things you can do to Challenge the Process that were suggested in module 5. Review them, pick one from the list to commit to, or define another way to practice Inspire a Shared Vision, and then describe what you will do to meet that commitment.

1. Make a list of tasks that you perform that are related to your various leadership activities. For each task, ask yourself, "Why am I doing this? Why am I doing it this way? Can this task be eliminated or done significantly better?" Based on your responses, do you see where you can develop other skills? Identify those skills and look for applicable opportunities within your leadership activities where you can work to develop the skills you have identified. (3, 8)

2. Make a list of the things your group does that are basically done the same way as they have always been done before. For each routine, ask, "Are we doing this at our best?" If yes, then carry on! If no, look for ways to change to make it better. (8, 18, 28)

3. Continue to observe and learn about what makes other leaders successful, and then think about your own skills. Which skills do you see those leaders having that you don't? Perhaps you believe you have those skills but need to strengthen them. Talk to those individuals and ask for their suggestions on what you could do to get stronger. If you don't have that opportunity, write down the skills or abilities you want to work on and ask an advisor, teacher, coach, or student life staff member to help you find places at your school or organization where you can develop those skills. (3, 13)

4. Ask others in your group what frustrates them about the organization. Make a commitment to change three of the most frequently mentioned items that are frustrating people and probably hindering the group's success. (13, 18)

5. Identify a process in your group that's not working, and take action to fix it. Learn from your experience. (18, 28)

6. Experiment by doing something you are not currently doing that will benefit your group—perhaps something new you can do within a project or event you are already working on. You might find something new you can do together that can meet a goal of your group. Make your experiments small, and learn from them for future larger experiments. (8, 28)

7. Eliminate "fire hosing" (throwing water on every new idea without giving it consideration). Remove from your group's vocabulary the "That'll never work" phrase or "The problem with that is . . ." At the very least, give new ideas the benefit of discussion and reflection. Recognize that even if the first idea isn't valuable, it might lead to others that are. (8, 18, 28)

8.   Call or visit your counterparts in other organizations at your school, another school or group, or another community (both those in groups similar to yours and different from yours). Find out what they are doing and learn from their successes and challenges. Copy what they do well and use their failures as a guide for improvement. (13)

9.   Set achievable goals. Tell people what the key milestones are and review them frequently so that you and they can easily see progress. (23)

10.   Eliminate the phrase, "That's the way we did it last year," from all discussions. Use the results of past programs or projects to learn from, but don't fall into the trap of doing something the same way simply because it's easier. (8, 23, 28)

Ways that I will practice Challenge the Process and how I will do that:

AFTER REVIEWING THE LEADERSHIP PRACTICE OF ENABLE OTHERS TO ACT

Take Action (What Do You Intend to Do?)

Use your Student LPI report and what you have learned about Enable Others to Act to take action based on one of the six leadership behaviors associated with this practice.

The leadership behavior I've chosen:

Your Actions

1.   To demonstrate this behavior from Enable Others to Act, the actions I need to take are:

2.   Detail how each element of a S.M.A.R.T. action is addressed in your action plan.

Specific: Is your action clear and simple? Does it answer the following questions?

What do you want to accomplish?

Who is involved?

When will it take place?

Where will it take place?

Measurable: Is there a clear way to measure completion or success?

Attainable/Action-Oriented: Can this goal be accomplished? How?

Relevant/Reasonable: Is this action relevant for the goal you have in mind as a leader? How?

Timely: Is a time frame attached? If so, what is it?

Look Within (What Did You Learn from Taking Action?)

1.   What happened when you took this action?

2.   What were the results of taking this action?

3. What did you learn about the value of demonstrating this behavior?

4. What parts of this action were comfortable and easy? What was difficult? What might your answers tell you about yourself as a leader?

Ongoing Learning (What Will You Do Next Based on This Experience?)

Refine your philosophy of leadership. With a deeper understanding of Enable Others to Act, is there anything you would like to add or revise in your answer to the question, "I want to be known as a leader who_____"?

Commit to deepening your practice. Following are examples of things you can do to Enable Others to Act that were suggested in module 6. Review them, pick one from the list to commit to, or define another way to practice Inspire a Shared Vision, and then describe what you will do to meet that commitment.

1. Teach others in your group to become leaders. Leaders bring others along to be leaders. Take some specific steps, perhaps starting with just one or two people, to help them develop their leadership abilities. (24, 29)

2. Make a point of encouraging others to take on important tasks or projects. Put the names forward of people on the team you believe would be well suited for a certain project. Similarly, talk with them about taking on a responsibility on behalf of the group, letting them know that you have confidence in their ability and judgment. (4, 14, 19, 24, 29)

3. Take another approach to item 2 by asking someone else to lead a group meeting or do a presentation so he or she can gain that experience (or any other experiences you identify). Then coach this person along the way to assist and support him or her in this new capacity. (4, 14, 24, 29)

4. Give something up altogether that you do on a regular basis. Don't just give up something you don't want to do, but find someone in the group you think would grow from taking over this task as a regular responsibility. Be sure to let him or her know that you are not just getting rid of something you no longer care to do or think is critical; rather, explain how this represents an opportunity for this person to grow and develop. (4, 9, 19, 24, 29)

5. Identify someone at your school or in your community who is known as an exceptional leader. Contact that person and find out if you can follow or shadow him or her for a few hours to learn about how you can become better in working with others. (4, 9, 14)

6. Improve relationships and develop a greater sense of trust with group members by doing something together outside regular group activities. Find ways to interact informally so you and they can build stronger bonds with each other. (4, 9, 14)

7. For the next two weeks, see how often you can replace "I" with "we" as you lead a group. Work to develop the philosophy and understanding that leadership is about the group or the team, not one individual. Every time you think about saying "I'm going to . . . ," say instead, "We can do this . . ." (4, 9, 14, 29)

8. Ask an athletic coach if you can watch a practice or team meeting to see how he or she helps athletes develop new skills or identify and reach new goals. Think about how you can apply these lessons to the groups to which you belong. (4, 9)

Ways that I will practice Enable Others to Act and how I will do that:

AFTER REVIEWING THE LEADERSHIP PRACTICE OF ENCOURAGE THE HEART

Take Action (What Do You Intend to Do?)

Use your Student LPI report and what you have learned about Encourage the Heart to take action based on one of the six leadership behaviors associated with this practice.

The leadership behavior I've chosen:

Your Actions

1. To demonstrate this behavior from Encourage the Heart, the actions I need to take are:

2. Detail how each element of a S.M.A.R.T. action is addressed in your action plan.

    Specific: Is your action clear and simple? Does it answer the following questions?

    What do you want to accomplish?

    Who is involved?

    When will it take place?

    Where will it take place?

    Measurable: Is there a clear way to measure completion or success?

    Attainable/Action-Oriented: Can this goal be accomplished? How?

    Relevant/Reasonable: Is this action relevant for the goal you have in mind as a leader? How?

    Timely: Is a time frame attached? If so, what is it?

Look Within (What Did You Learn from Taking Action?)

1. What happened when you took this action?
2. What were the results of taking this action?
3. What did you learn about the value of demonstrating this behavior?
4. What parts of this action were comfortable and easy? What was difficult? What might your answers tell you about yourself as a leader?

Ongoing Learning (What Will You Do Next Based on This Experience?)

Refine your philosophy of leadership. With a deeper understanding of Encourage the Heart, is there anything you would like to add or revise in your answer to the question, "I want to be known as a leader who_____"?

Commit to deepening your practice. Following are examples of things you can do to Encourage the Heart that were suggested in module 7. Review them, pick one from the list to commit to, or define another way to practice Inspire a Shared Vision, and then describe what you will do to meet that commitment.

1. If your group is working on a larger project or event, identify small milestones along the way that would be appropriate places for you to celebrate. Don't wait until the entire project is finished. Celebrating your success and progress along the way will encourage others to keep going. (10, 25)

2. As often as you can, share a story publicly with the group or other appropriate audiences about someone in the group who did something exceptional; that is, that person went above and beyond the call of duty. (5, 10, 15, 20, 30)

3. When recognizing someone, think of the "three Ws": who, what, and why. Recognize the person by name (*who*). Describe *what* the person did. You don't need to go into immense detail, but share enough of the story so others can see how exceptional the work was. Finally, tell *why* what the person did mattered to the group. Connect this person's work to the values of the organization to demonstrate that you recognize how he or she is truly making a difference to make the group better. (5, 20, 30)

4. Use informal times and gatherings to find out what others are doing that exemplify what the group stands for. Take a moment to recognize these people on the spot. (10, 20, 30)

5. When you talk with someone in the group and are getting to know him or her, find out what encourages this person. Ask how he or she likes to be recognized and what has meaning for him or her. You might ask about times in the past when something special was done for that person and what that meant. When the time comes, you will be prepared to recognize this person in a meaningful way. (5, 10, 15, 30)

6. Write at least three thank-you notes every week to those who are doing work (taking actions) that supports and improves the group. (5, 15, 30)

7. If you receive or hear acknowledgments of good work from others about people in your group, be sure to pass those comments along to them in a public way. You might read the note aloud at a meeting, put it on your group's website, or release it through social media. (5, 20, 25, 30)

8. Be on the lookout for creative gifts you can use to recognize and reward people. You can find inexpensive things in retail stores that you can easily relate a story to. You

can also use things you might come across, such as photos, buttons, small stuffed animals, painted rocks, ribbons, or some other trinkets. It is not the gift but the thought and the story that goes with the gift that matter the most. (5, 10, 15, 30)

9. Create some tools anyone in the group can use to recognize others at any time. Preprint some note cards or pads, for example, or come up with a unique award or something that you can turn into a tradition for the group that others can give to someone doing exceptional work. (25, 30)

10. If you do have end-of-term or end-of-school-year activities, go beyond the typical certificate or plaque and be sure to put personal stories behind the recognition. If someone has been doing extraordinary work and really made an impact on the group, acknowledge those contributions by sharing them with the audience. You give greater meaning to the contributions by sharing an individual story about the individual. (5, 15, 20, 25, 30)

Ways that I will practice Encourage the Heart and how I will do that:

MODULE 9

Sample Student Leadership Development Curricula

We've written this *Facilitation and Activities Guide* to be as flexible as possible. Rather than guide you and your students through a prescribed workshop, our intention is to offer you the tools you need to blend The Five Practices of Exemplary Leadership model into the work you're already doing, so that it contributes to your desired learning outcomes. Although the model can be taught as a complete program, it can also be used as a guiding framework or a supplement to your existing curricula, program, or class activities.

This Module offers suggested curricula to help get you started if you are teaching leadership development in any of the following formats:

- A series of cocurricular classes or workshops over time
- An academic course
- A one-day workshop or retreat

These suggestions are not rigid. Use them as guidelines, and modify them as appropriate to your context.

SEVEN-SESSION COCURRICULAR WORKSHOP SERIES

This cocurricular series is designed as seven one-hour workshops.

By participating in this workshop, students will:

- Develop an understanding that leadership can be learned
- Be able to describe The Five Practices of Exemplary Leadership
- Apply specific strategies to develop their personal leadership behavior

This key applies to all sessions: SW-*Student Workbook*, FG-*Facilitator Guide*, TSLC-*The Student Leadership Challenge* book, PLJ-Personal Leadership Journal.

Session 1: Introduction and Overview

Length of Segment	Cumulative Elapsed Time	Topic	Related Work/Resources
Prework		Assign the personal-best leadership experience and the Student LPI Online 2 to 3 weeks prior to the first workshop	Alternative: assign the personal best in the first session to be discussed in session 2. Assign the Student LPI Self (paper) TSLC: Five Practices of Exemplary Leadership, Truths about Leadership FG, SW: Activity 1.1 and Module 2

5 minutes	5 minutes	1. Welcome and introductions 2. Overview and objectives of the workshop	
30 minutes	35 minutes	1. Five Practices Overview of the Student Leadership Challenge model and impact on personal leadership development 2. Core concepts 3. Personal Leadership Journal 4. Student LPI results (if completed as prework)	FG, SW: Module 1, Introduction Facilitator cue: Allot more time here if you are reviewing the Student LPI results
20 minutes	55 minutes	Personal-Best Leadership Experience, Activity 1.1	FG, SW
5 minutes	60 minutes	Transition/introduction to session 2	

Session 2: Model the Way

Length of Segment	Cumulative Elapsed Time	Topic	Related Work/Resources
Previous work		Personal best unless done as prework or in session 1	TSLC: Model the Way Consider assigning material in the PLJ
5 minutes	5 minutes	1. Overview and objectives of the workshop 2. Reflections and questions on session 1, core concepts Add: Group introductions again	
15 minutes	20 minutes	Discuss the Student LPI results (if not done in session 1) Add: Alternative content if students already have debriefed the Student LPI results	FG: Module 2, Interpreting the Student LPI Results; use in conjunction with the PLJ
35 minutes	55 minutes	1. Leadership practice: Model the Way 2. Activity 3.2: Mark Your Calendars	TSLC: Model the Way FG, SW: Module 3, Model the Way
5 minutes	60 minutes	Transition/introduction to session 3	

Session 3: Inspire a Shared Vision

Length of Segment	Cumulative Elapsed Time	Topic	Related Work/Resources
Previous work			TSLC: Inspire a Shared Vision Consider assigning material in the PLJ
5 minutes	5 minutes	1. Overview and objectives of the workshop 2. Reflections and questions on session 2, Model the Way	Facilitator cue: If the PLJ is used in this series, check in at the beginning of each session on progress
50 minutes	55 minutes	1. Leadership practice: Inspire a Shared Vision 2. Activity 4.2: Come Join Me on Vacation	TSLC: Inspire a Shared Vision FG, SW: Module 4, Inspire a Shared Vision
5 minutes	60 minutes	Transition/introduction to session 4	

Session 4: Challenge the Process

Length of Segment	Cumulative Elapsed Time	Topic	Related Work/Resources
Previous work			TSLC: Challenge the Process Consider assigning material in the PLJ
5 minutes	5 minutes	1. Overview and objectives of the workshop 2. Reflections and questions on session 3. Inspire a Shared Vision	
50 minutes	55 minutes	1. Leadership practice: Challenge the Process 2. Activity 5.3: Movie Activity: *Apollo 13*	TSLC: Challenge the Process FG, SW: Module 5, Challenge the Process
5 minutes	60 minutes	Transition/introduction to session 5	

Session 5: Enable Others to Act

Length of Segment	Cumulative Elapsed Time	Topic	Related Work/Resources
Previous work			TSLC: Enable Others to Act Consider assigning material in the PLJ
5 minutes	5 minutes	1. Overview and objectives of the workshop 2. Reflections and questions on session 4, Challenge the Process	
50 minutes	55 minutes	1. Leadership practice: Enable Others to Act 2. Activity 6.1: What Makes You Trust Someone?	TSLC: Enable Others to Act FG, SW: Module 6, Enable Others to Act
5 minutes	60 minutes	Transition/introduction to session 6	

Session 6: Encourage the Heart

Length of Segment	Cumulative Elapsed Time	Topic	Related Work/ Resources
Previous work			TSLC: Encourage the Heart Consider assigning material in the PLJ
5 minutes	5 minutes	1. Overview and objectives of the workshop 2. Reflections and questions on session 5, Enable Others to Act	
50 minutes	55 minutes	1. Leadership practice: Encourage the Heart 2. Activity 7.2: Recognition Cards	TSLC: Encourage the Heart FG: Module 7, Encourage the Heart
5 minutes	60 minutes	Transition/introduction to session 7	

Session 7: Into Action

Length of Segment	Cumulative Elapsed Time	Topic	Related Work/Resources
Previous work		None	
5 minutes	5 minutes	1. Overview and objectives of the workshop 2. Reflections and questions on session 6, Encourage the Heart	
35 minutes	40 minutes	Facilitator guides discussion on next steps students can take using their PLJ and further actions they can take with The Five Practices. Use data from the Student LPI as well as revisit the personal-best leadership experience stories to look for areas in which to concentrate.	TSLC: Revisit Truths about Leadership, Five Practices of Exemplary Leadership FG, SW: Personal Best, Student LPI, PLJ
20 minutes	60 minutes	Celebration of community and completion of program	Facilitator determines appropriate way to celebrate the conclusion of the workshop series. Consider the ways to practice the behaviors in Encourage the Heart to guide your planning.

SAMPLE ACADEMIC COURSE CURRICULUM: SIX-WEEK MODULE

This six-week sample course curriculum is structured for a class that meets twice weekly for seventy-five minutes each session. This curriculum is designed so that it can be infused in any course on leadership. We offer some suggestions about how to expand on this design for a ten-week or quarter-system course following the syllabus.

Sample Learning Outcomes

By participating in this course, students will:

- Understand the fundamental principles of leadership development
- Be able to identify the characteristics of exceptional leaders
- Identify The Five Practices of Exemplary Leadership
- Distinguish specific leadership behaviors they and others have
- Practice specific behaviors correlated with exemplary leadership performance
- Design a personal action plan for developing their leadership behavior
- Integrate specific leadership habits into their daily activities
- Evaluate their progress in developing as a leader
- Understand strategies to help others develop their leadership behaviors

This key applies to all sessions: SW-*Student Workbook*, FG-*Facilitator Guide*, TSLC-*The Student Leadership Challenge* book, PLJ-Personal Leadership Journal.

Date	Topic/Subject	Related Work/Resources
Week 1, class 1	First session of the class module 1. Introduction and overview of The Student Leadership Challenge model and The Five Practices of Exemplary Leadership 2. Personal definition of leadership 3. Instructions and administration of the student leadership practices Inventory (Student LPI)	Assignments 1. Write a personal definition of leadership to compare to others in the class to identify similarities and differences in understanding what leadership is. 2. Student leadership practices Inventory with minimum of eight observers, complete by fifth class meeting 3. Personal best leadership experience 4. TSLC: Five Practices of Exemplary Leadership, Truths about Leadership 5. FG, SW: Modules 1, 2
Week 1, class 2	Personal-best leadership experience	FG, SW: personal-best leadership experience TSLC: Five Practices of Exemplary Leadership, Truths about Leadership
Week 2, class 1	Core concepts	FG: Module 1 TSLC: Chapters 1, 2, 8
Week 2, class 2	Leadership practice: Model the Way Activity 3.3: Movie Activity: *Pay It Forward*. Watch entire movie. Requires two classes or outside assignment.	FG, SW: Module 3 TSLC: Model the Way Facilitator cue: Begin Model the Way with Activity 3.3. Content will be taught in the following week as noted.

(Continued)

Continued

Date	Topic/Subject	Related Work/Resources
Week 3, class 1	Understanding the Student Leadership Practices Inventory. Provide reports and discuss results Overview of developing a personal leadership journal	FG, SW: Module 2 Student LPI reports
Week 3, class 2	Leadership practice: Model the Way teaching Activity 3.3: Movie Activity: *Pay It Forward* discussion Activities 3.1 and 3.2: Values Spotlight and Mark Your Calendars	FG, SW: Module 3 TSLC: Model the Way Incorporate Model the Way strategies into the PLJ
Week 4, class 1	Leadership practice: Inspire a Shared Vision teaching Activities 4.1 and 4.2: The Dream Sheet and Come Join Me on Vacation Optional activity: Activity 4.3: Movie Activity: *Invictus*	FG, SW: Module 4 TSLC: Inspire a Shared Vision Incorporate Inspire a Shared Vision strategies into the PLJ
Week 4, class 2	Leadership practice: Challenge the Process teaching Activities 5.1 and 5.2: We Need More Parking and Take It One Step at a Time Optional activity: Activity 5.3: Movie Activity: *Apollo 13*	FG, SW: Module 5 TSLC: Challenge the Process Incorporate Challenge the Process strategies into the PLJ
Week 5, class 1	Leadership practice: Enable Others to Act teaching Activities 6.1 and 6.2: What Makes You Trust Someone? and Blindfolded Square Optional activity: Activity 6.3: Movie Activity: *Freedom Writers*	FG, SW: Module 6 TSLC: Enable Others to Act Incorporate Enable Others to Act strategies into the PLJ
Week 5, class 2	Leadership practice: Encourage the Heart teaching Activities 7.1 and 7.2: Web of Appreciation and Recognition Cards Optional activity: Activity 7.3: Movie Activity: *Harry Potter and the Sorcerer's Stone*	FG, SW: Module 7 TSLC: Encourage the Heart Incorporate Encourage the Heart strategies into the PLJ

Week 6, class 1	Build and review a final personal leadership journal	FG, SW: Module 8 *Facilitator cue:* As the personal leadership journals were created over the course of these classes, students should now review their plan in its entirety and reference their data from the Student LPI to adjust their plans accordingly. We recommend that students have an accountability partner in their class who can help them stay on track with their leadership growth. Educators can also build in accountability at other points throughout the leadership course.
Week 6, class 2	Final project options: *Facilitator cue:* As stated in Module 1, this model of leadership is about behavior and action. Although the content teaching has concluded, we recommend that educators use this final class session to assign one of the suggested project ideas and create time later in the course to revisit the project where applicable. The application of the model through these experiences will help students develop their capacity as a leader through increased frequency of effective leadership behaviors in The Five Practices.	Optional in-class project: Group Presentation on aspect of The Five Practices of Exemplary Leadership Optional in-class project: Paper assignment on The Five Practices Optional in-class project: Reflection on Student LPI Optional in-class project: Case studies on group development related to establishing relationships, collaboration, group and individual trust, or other related topic Optional continuing project: Service project Optional continuing project: Integration of The Five Practices into club, organization, or team

Expanding the Syllabus

This syllabus could easily be expanded to fit a ten-week or quarter-system course in several ways. For example, you could invite guest speakers to share their experiences about leading, how they learned about leadership, and what they think it takes to be an effective leader. These speakers do not necessarily need to be familiar with The Five Practices framework; indeed, it is interesting to discuss with the students afterward how the speaker's remarks are consistent, or not, with the model. You can invite people from your campus (e.g., the dean, president, athletic director, coach, student personnel officers, student government officers) or from the community. Alumni (and donors!) always like to come to campus and share their experiences. You could also invite more than one speaker to a class session and use a panel format. The selection and recruitment of guest speakers can be delegated to the class.

Having the students work together in small groups to complete a project relevant to the course and then present their experiences to the rest of the class is another way to extend the number of class sessions. For example, each group could be responsible for holding a fundraiser for their designated charity. They could write a paper about the group dynamics of this experience and evaluate the leadership evident (their own and that of others). Each group could be assigned to one of The Five Practices and be charged with developing a three- to four-minute video that illustrates the key points of that leadership practice and present it to the class. You can find a number of these already circulating on YouTube. An alternative to a video would be having the small group develop (and perform) a role play or skit. In these ways, each small group could be charged with creating a learning experience for their classmates with the intention of helping fellow students become better in one of The Five Practices of Exemplary Leadership.

Another available resource is *The Leadership Challenge* DVD, a two-hour video that features up-to-date footage of Jim Kouzes and Barry Posner reflecting on The Five Practices of Exemplary Leadership model and their more than thirty years of research behind it. This story is interspersed with ten case studies, each especially indicative of one particular practice, along with three international case studies (one from the United Kingdom and two from Asia). Although the cases do not feature students, they do give students the chance to see what these leadership practices look like in the real world. You can show students one or more of these video cases and ask them to identify the ways in which that leader is engaging in any of The Five Practices. The videos help to make the leadership practices come alive.

ONE-DAY WORKSHOP OR RETREAT

This is a nine-hour program (with seven and a half hours of content).

By participating in this workshop, students will:

- Understand the fundamental principles of leadership development
- Be able to identify the characteristics of exceptional leaders
- Identify The Five Practices of Exemplary Leadership
- Distinguish specific leadership behaviors they and others have
- Practice specific behaviors correlated with exemplary leadership performance
- Design a personal action plan for developing their leadership behavior

This key applies to all sessions: SW-*Student Workbook*, FG-*Facilitator Guide*, TSLC-*The Student Leadership Challenge* book, PLJ-Personal Leadership Journal.

Length of Segment	Cumulative Elapsed Time	Topic	Related Work/Resources
Prework		Have students complete the Student LPI Online (or paper version), with a minimum of eight observer respondents—submit in advance to facilitator Note: if paper version is used, advance time may need to be increased Complete Activity 1.1: Personal-Best Leadership Experience narrative; bring to workshop	To be assigned three to four weeks prior to the workshop. Student LPI reports created and delivered at the workshop Alternative: Provide the paper version of the Student LPI Self and administer it at the beginning of the workshop. This will give students a start with their self-awareness of leadership, but will not give them a full 360-degree understanding of their leadership behavior. FG, SW
45 minutes	45 minutes	1. Registration check-in, welcome and introductions 2. Overview of the workshop schedule 3. Expectations of the day 4. Ice breaker (for a new group); team builder or extended introduction (for an established group)	
45 minutes	1 hour, 30 minutes	Personal-best leadership experience reflections	Small groups discuss person-best leadership experience, reactions, commonalities, relevance to leadership. FG, SW: Module 1
45 minutes	1 hour, 45 minutes	Core concepts teaching	FG: Module 1
15 minutes	2 hours	Break	

(Continued)

Continued

Length of Segment	Cumulative Elapsed Time	Topic	Related Work/Resources
15 minutes	2 hours, 15 minutes	Overview of personal leadership journal	FG, SW: Module 8
45 minutes	3 hours	Student LPI overview and explanation	FG: Module 2 Distribute Student LPI reports
60 minutes	4 hours	1. Model overview: Introduce concepts of Five Practices and 10 Commitments (20 minutes) 2. Leadership practice: Model the Way Teaching (40 minutes) 3. Activity 3.1: Values Spotlight	FG, SW – Modules 1, 3 Facilitator Cue: Note that some activities may need to be shortened depending on your actual schedule.
60	5 hours	Lunch	
40 minutes	5 hours, 40 minutes	1. Leadership practice: Inspire a Shared Vision 2. Activity 4.1: The Dream Sheet	FG, SW: Module 4
40 minutes	6 hours, 20 minutes	1. Leadership practice: Challenge the Process 2. Activity 5.1: We Need More Parking	FG, SW: Module 5
40 minutes	7 hours	1. Leadership practice: Enable Others to Act 2. Activity 6.2: Blindfolded Square	FG, SW: Module 6
20 minutes	7 hours, 20 minutes	Break	
40 minutes	8 hours	1. Leadership practice: Encourage the Heart 2. Activities 7.1 and 7.2: Web of Appreciation and Recognition Cards	FG, SW: Module 7 Facilitator cue: Activity 7.1 can be used as a closing activity and Activity 7.2 can be given to students to do after the workshop.

30 minutes	8 hours, 30 minutes	1. Student LPI reflection 2. Personal Leadership Journal	FG, SW: Modules 2 and 9 Facilitator cue: Have students develop a specific piece that they will work on in the next week and then use the PLJ for long-term growth.
15 minutes	8 hours, 45 minutes	Wrap-up, evaluation, final questions	Evaluation Optional closing commitment activity: Have students state the one thing they will do to concentrate on a specific behavior next week (Personal Leadership Journal commitment).

ONWARD!

At the end of any leadership development effort with your students, from an hour's conversation, a one-day workshop, weekly seminar, or complete academic term course, you need to (drum roll, please!) Encourage the Heart. You are the one helping these young people find themselves and face their uncertainties, and you are motivating them to take action long after they have left your presence. You're like the director in the theater who prepares the cast, takes them through rehearsals, and after opening night is no longer present (at least physically so). When the workshop, seminar, or class is over, the students are on their own to be the better leaders that you have helped them to become.

Make sure that you send them on their way knowing of your faith and confidence in them, and with your very best wishes for their success in every leadership adventure. Put it into your own words, of course, but in the "Onward!" conclusion to the *Student Workbook and Personal Leadership Journal,* this is exactly our intention. We reprint it here:

• • •

Congratulations for navigating your way through this workbook! However far you made it through the many suggestions, activities, and reflections in it, you should feel great about yourself. We've tried to make leadership simple to understand and shown what it looks like in practice, but simple doesn't mean that it is easy to be a leader or to learn how to become an even better leader.

No one is perfect. Every leader has flaws, and no one gets it right the first time or even every time. In sports, we see how professionals make the difficult look easy and how amateurs make the easy look difficult. Being professional is an ongoing endeavor no matter the sport, the setting, or the situation. Being a leader is no different. Despite your best efforts and most noble intentions, things won't always work out as you hoped, people will not always do what they promised or are capable of, and forces beyond your control will derail your plans.

Perhaps the truest test of leadership is in people's ability to bounce back from defeat and adversity, to pick themselves up and try again. History shows us that this quality of resilience is characteristic of all great leaders, and deeper analyses show that this stems from their being both clear and committed to a set of values and way of being. Becoming a better leader, as we indicated at the onset, begins with clarifying your values, finding your voice, and conscientiously aligning your actions with shared values.

We first talked about leadership with Melissa Poe when she was nine years old. Melissa was concerned about the environment, and as she took action at that young age and heard from other kids who were as concerned as she was, she started a club for kids and by kids. Starting with just six members at her elementary school, Kids F.A.C.E. (for a clean environment) grew to more than 2,000 club chapters in twenty-two countries and more than 350,000 members during the time Melissa was president. (Today there are 500,000 members.) At age seventeen, she stepped aside, joined the board, and handed over the reins to two fifteen year olds, saying she was too old for the job. She wanted the organization to always be in kids' hands.

When we caught up with Melissa almost twenty-five years later, she told us, "I believe everyone struggles with life purpose; however, a leader is one who steps beyond her own self-doubts and realizes her journey is her responsibility. Whether one is a child or an adult, an individual participates in the world, and she should do so deliberately. Ultimately the worst thing one can do is to see a problem and think it is someone else's responsibility."

Melissa reminds us that leadership is not about wishful thinking. It's about determined doing. There are no shortages of problems and opportunities at school, at home, in our neighborhoods, at work, and around the globe. There are no shortages of problems to solve. Leadership is not about telling others that they ought to solve these problems. It's about seeing a problem and accepting personal responsibility for doing something about it. And it's about holding yourself accountable for the actions that you take. The next time you see a problem and say, "Why doesn't someone do something about this?" take a look in the mirror and say instead, "I'll be the someone to do something about it."

This doesn't mean that you have to accept responsibility for every problem, and it doesn't mean that you should solve problems you see by yourself. What it does mean is that leaders are active participants who work tirelessly to mobilize others to want to work for shared aspirations. They are not bystanders in the parade of life. Leaders believe that they have an obligation to do something to bring about change and that they can move things forward with the active engagement of others.

You make a difference. Don't let anyone or anything that happens persuade you otherwise. You'll be amazed by how many opportunities you have every day to act as a leader and make a difference. And you'll be pleasantly surprised by how much improvement you will be able to make by being more conscientious and intentional about acting as a leader.

APPENDIX A

Student Leadership Practices Inventory Behavior Statements

Here are the six behavior statements from the Student Leadership Practices Inventory products for each of The Five Practices of Exemplary Leadership. The first iteration of the statement is the exact behavior. The iteration in parentheses is the way the behavior statement appears in the individual reports for the Student LPI 360 and Student LPI Self Online.

Model the Way Statements

1 "I set a personal example of what I expect from other people." ("Sets personal example.")

6 "I spend time making sure that people behave consistently with the principles and standards we have agreed upon." ("Aligns others with principles and standards.")

11 "I follow through on the promises and commitments I make." ("Follows through on promises.")

16 "I seek to understand how my actions affect other people's performance." ("Seeks feedback about impact of actions.")

21 "I make sure that people support the values we have agreed upon." ("Makes sure people support common values.")

26 "I talk about my values and the principles that guide my actions." ("Talks about values and principles.")

Inspire a Shared Vision Statements

2 "I look ahead and communicate what I believe will affect us in the future." ("Looks ahead and communicates future.")

7 "I describe to others in our organization what we should be capable of accomplishing." ("Describes ideal capabilities.")

12 "I talk with others about a vision of how things could be even better in the future." ("Talks about how future could be better.")

17 "I talk with others about how their own interests can be met by working toward a common goal." ("Shows others how their interests can be realized.")

22 "I am upbeat and positive when talking about what we can accomplish." ("Is upbeat and positive.")

27 "I speak with passion about the higher purpose and meaning of what we are doing." ("Communicates purpose and meaning.")

Challenge the Process Statements

3 "I look for ways to develop and challenge my skills and abilities." ("Challenges skills and abilities.")

8 "I look for ways that others can try out new ideas and methods." ("Helps others try out new ideas.")

13 "I search for innovative ways to improve what we are doing." ("Searches for innovative ways to improve.")

18 "When things don't go as we expected, I ask, 'What can we learn from this experience?'" ("Asks, 'What can we learn?'")

23 "I make sure that big projects we undertake are broken down into smaller and doable parts." ("Breaks projects into smaller doable portions.")

28 "I take initiative in experimenting with the way things can be done." ("Takes initiative in experimenting.")

Enable Others to Act Statements

4 "I foster cooperative rather than competitive relationships among people I work with." ("Fosters cooperative relationships.")

9 "I actively listen to diverse points of view." ("Actively listens to diverse viewpoints.")

14 "I treat others with dignity and respect." ("Treats others with respect.")

19 "I support the decisions that other people make on their own." ("Supports decisions other people make.")

24 "I give others a great deal of freedom and choice in deciding how to do their work." ("Gives people choice about how to do their work.")

29 "I provide opportunities for others to take on leadership responsibilities." ("Provides leadership opportunities for others.")

Encourage the Heart Statements

5 "I praise people for a job well done." ("Praises people.")

10 "I encourage others as they work on activities and programs." ("Encourages others.")

15 "I express appreciation for the contributions that people make." ("Expresses appreciation for people's contributions.")

20 "I make it a point to publicly recognize people who show commitment to shared values." ("Publicly recognizes alignment with values.")

25 "I find ways for us to celebrate accomplishments." ("Celebrates accomplishments.")

30 "I make sure that people are creatively recognized for their contributions." ("Creatively recognizes people's contributions.")

APPENDIX B

Ten Tips for Becoming a Better Leader

We asked students and leadership coaches to share with us their best learning practices for becoming a better leader. We combined their observations with our own and others' research and summarized these lessons into the following ten tips. Think about how these apply to your own leadership development journey.

TIP 1: BE SELF-AWARE

The best leaders are highly aware of what's going on inside of them as they are leading. They're also very aware of the impact they're having on others. Think about it this way. Let's say you start falling behind in a class. You tell yourself you can catch up easily, so you ignore a couple of low grades on spot quizzes. Then one day you realize that the midterm is coming up and you haven't cracked a book in weeks. That you ignored the work for so long is going to cost you a lot in terms of time and grades.

The same is true in leading. Self-awareness gives you clues about what's going on inside you and in your environment. If you ignore those clues, you might find it difficult or impossible to catch up.

Your feelings are messages that are trying to teach you something. So, listen and learn, take time to reflect on your experiences, and keep a journal. As you go through your developmental experiences, look within yourself and pay attention to how you're feeling.

TIP 2: MANAGE YOUR EMOTIONS

The best leaders are careful not to let their feelings manage them. Instead, they manage their feelings.

Let's say that you tend to get angry when people come unprepared for a meeting. You could express your anger and put them down in front of the group. But would that be the best way to handle the situation? Common sense says that it wouldn't. The better choice would be to be aware of your anger, acknowledge it, and then decide on the most effective way to deal with the problem. The same is true in learning.

Sometimes you will feel frustrated and upset by the feedback that you receive. You might even feel angry at the person who gave you the feedback. Be aware of your feelings, but don't let them rule your behavior. If you sense that you need help managing your emotions, seek it from a trusted teacher, advisor, counselor, family member, or cleric.

TIP 3: SEEK FEEDBACK

The best leaders ask for feedback from others—feedback not only about what they're doing well but about what they're not doing well. That's one reason why managing your emotions is so important. No one is going to give you negative feedback if you're likely to get angry. Let people know that you genuinely want their feedback, and then do something with the feedback they give you. Afterward, ask, "How'd I do?" Have a conversation. Then say thanks.

TIP 4: TAKE THE INITIATIVE

The Leadership Challenge research is clear on this point: the best leaders don't wait for someone else to tell them what to do. They take the initiative to find and solve problems and to meet and create challenges. The same is true in learning: the best leaders take charge of their own learning. Because they're self-aware and seek feedback, they know their strengths and weaknesses, and they know what they need to learn. They find a way to get the experience, example, or education they need. It's your learning, your life. Take charge of it.

TIP 5: SEEK HELP

Top athletes, musicians, and performing artists all have coaches. Leadership is a performing art too, and it never hurts to have some help. Ask a teacher or mentor you respect to watch you perform, give you feedback, offer suggestions for improvement, and give you support generally. In your school or organization, there is an abundance of people you could ask to help coach you. Look to your group advisors, teachers, and faculty members you feel connected to; career centers and counseling centers might offer personal development services too. You can also consider fellow students and friends whom you feel have great leadership experiences. If you are employed, consider a coworker or supervisor. You might find yourself working with a couple of coaches who have expertise in different areas you want to explore.

TIP 6: SET GOALS AND MAKE A PLAN

If you have a clear sense of what you want to accomplish, you'll be much more likely to apply what you learn. Leaders who are successful at bringing out the best in themselves and in others set achievable stretch goals—goals that are high but not so far out of reach that people give up even before they start.

It's also important to make your goals public. You will work harder to improve when you've told others what you're trying to accomplish.

Once you've set goals, make a plan. There may be several ways to get from where you are to where you want to be, just as there are several routes you could take to travel across the country. Pick the one that best suits your needs.

When you make your plan, remember that journeys are completed one step at a time. It's the same with leadership development. You may have a strong desire to improve in three of The Five Practices of Exemplary Leadership and in ten of the thirty behaviors. That's terrific, but don't try to do everything at once. Take it bit by bit. There is no such thing as overnight success in becoming an exemplary leader.

TIP 7: PRACTICE, PRACTICE, PRACTICE

People who practice often are more likely to become experts at what they do than those who don't practice or do so only fitfully. We know this is true in the arts and in sports, but the same idea hasn't always been applied to leadership.

Practice is essential to learning. Practice might be rehearsing a speech or a new way of running a meeting. It might be sitting down with a friend to try out a conversation you plan to have with a member of your group.

Whatever it is, practice gives you the chance to become comfortable with and try out new methods, behaviors, and strategies in a safe environment. In fact, every experience is a form of practice, even when it's for real. Whether the experience is a raving success or a miserable failure, ask yourself and those involved, "What went well? What went poorly?" "What did I do well? What did I do poorly?" "What could I improve?" The best leaders are the best learners, and learning can occur at any time and anywhere.

TIP 8: MEASURE PROGRESS

You need to know whether you're making progress or marking time. It's not enough to know that you want to make it to the summit and how to recognize that summit once you're there. You also need to know whether you're still climbing or sliding downhill.

Measuring progress is crucial to improvement no matter what the activity—strengthening endurance, shedding pounds, or becoming a better leader. The best measurement systems are ones that are visible and instant—like the speedometer on your dashboard or the watch on your wrist. For instance, you can count how many thank-you notes you send out by keeping a log. A self-monitoring system can include asking for feedback. Another way to monitor your progress is to take the Student LPI more than once.

TIP 9: REWARD YOURSELF

Connect your performance to rewards. It's nice when others recognize you for your efforts, but that doesn't always happen. So along with the goals that you set and the measurement system that you put in place, create some ways to reward yourself for achieving your goals. Give yourself a night off to go to a movie or a party with a friend. Buy yourself something you'd like; it doesn't have to be expensive. Mark the achievement in red pen on your calendar. Brag about it.

You can also schedule rewards when you reach milestones. Having a learning buddy is much like how endurance sports training program Team in Training helps people prepare to run marathons and triathlons to raise money for blood cancers.

TIP 10: BE HONEST WITH YOURSELF AND HUMBLE WITH OTHERS

We know from The Leadership Challenge research that credibility is the foundation of leadership and honesty is at the top of the list of what constituents look for in a leader. But what does honesty have to do with learning to lead? Everything. The ongoing research has yet to produce a leader who scores a perfect 30 on every leadership practice. Everyone can improve, and the first step is understanding, and acknowledging, what needs improving.

Being honest means that you're willing to admit mistakes, own up to your faults, and be open to suggestions for improvement. It also means that you're accepting of the same in others.

Honesty with yourself and others produces a level of humility that earns you credibility. People don't respect know-it-alls, especially when the know-it-all doesn't know it all. Admitting mistakes and being open to new ideas and new learning communicates that you are willing to grow. It promotes a culture of honesty and openness that's healthy for you and for others.

Hubris, that is, excessive pride, is the killer disease in leadership. It's fun to be a leader, gratifying to have influence, and exhilarating when people cheer your every word. But it's easy to be seduced by power and importance. Humility is the only way to resolve the conflicts and contradictions of leadership. Excessive pride can be avoided only if you recognize that you're human and need the help of others. That in itself is an important reason for leaders being great learners.

ACKNOWLEDGMENTS

Of all the leadership lessons we have learned over the years, the one that most needs repeating at the end of a project is this one: "You can't do it alone." Leadership is not a solo performance; it's a collaborative effort. And so is writing, editing, and producing a guide such as this one. We—Jim, Barry, Beth, and Gary—couldn't have done this without the expertise, dedication, and caring of the wonderful team of exceptional people who made this possible.

First off, the only reason we were able to create *The Student Leadership Challenge Facilitation and Activity Guide* is because of the gracious support of our good colleagues in colleges, universities, secondary schools, and community organizations who have dedicated themselves to developing emerging leaders. Their commitment to student leadership is inspiring, and their acceptance of our research, content, and methods has truly encouraged our hearts. We gratefully acknowledge the administrators, educators, and students who contributed their creative ideas and personal stories to this volume—and to our understanding of the dynamics of leadership in their settings.

We've enjoyed a three-decades-long partnership with our publisher, Jossey-Bass, an imprint of John Wiley & Sons. We've been a team since the beginning, and it's always a great joy to collaborate with them.

A very loud shout-out goes to our editor, Erin Null. Erin has been the champion of all *The Student Leadership Challenge* materials, and she is continuously encouraging and driving us to improve how we present our work. Erin made this revised edition happen, and she has been our guiding star on this project. Paul Foster, vice president and publisher of the Jossey-Bass higher education team, and Debra Hunter, president of Jossey-Bass and Pfeiffer imprints, have been constant sponsors of this work. Without them, we wouldn't have the resources to go from concept to distribution.

Other key members of the Jossey-Bass Higher Education Team were instrumental to the successful completion of this work. Alison Knowles, assistant editor, Bev Miller, copyeditor, and Cathy Mallon, content manager, skillfully navigated this guide through each iteration, making important improvements along the way. Others at Jossey-Bass were key to bringing this book into, and through, production and into the market. We offer our special thanks to Adrian Morgan, cover designer, and Aneesa Davenport, marketing manager, for their contributions in creating a product that others would want to open and use. For many years now Leslie Stephen has been the developmental editor on many of our books. She brings clarity and focus to our writing, and she challenges us, directly and indirectly, to improve what we say and how we say it. We truly appreciate how she makes everything she touches better.

At the beginning of each day when we begin our work, and at the end of the day when we shut down the computer for a little rest, it's our families who are there to share their love and support. We are blessed with their generous encouragement, helpful feedback, and constructive coaching. Jim and Barry are two very lucky guys to have extraordinary partners in Tae Kouzes and Jackie Schmidt-Posner. They also want to thank Nicholas Lopez, Jim's stepson; Amanda Posner, Barry's daughter; and Darryl Collins, Barry's son-in-law, for the inspiration and perspective they've provided. Beth thanks her husband, Tom, daughter, Georgia, and son, Evan, for their patience and support. Gary thanks Savannah, Sheri, Dell, and God for the support and inspiration to be a part of writing this book with Jim, Barry, and Beth.

With all these very special people in our lives, it drives home how true it is that leadership is an affair of the heart.

ABOUT THE AUTHORS

Jim Kouzes and Barry Posner have been working together for more than thirty years, studying leaders, researching leadership, conducting leadership development seminars, and serving as leaders themselves in various capacities. They are coauthors of the award-winning, best-selling book *The Leadership Challenge.* Since its first edition in 1987, *The Leadership Challenge* has sold more than 2 million copies worldwide and is available in more than twenty languages. It has been on the best-seller lists of *Business Week*, *Fortune*, and Amazon.com, and received numerous awards, including the Critics' Choice Award from the nation's book review editors, the James A. Hamilton Award for the outstanding management or health care book of the year, selected as one of the top ten books on leadership in Jack Covert and Todd Sattersten's *Top 100 Business Books of All Time*, and *FAST COMPANY* made it one of its top dozen business books of 2012.

Jim and Barry have coauthored more than a dozen other award-winning leadership books, including *Credibility: How Leaders Gain and Lose It, Why People Demand It; The Truth About Leadership: The No-Fads, Heart-of-the-Matter Facts You Need to Know; A Leader's Legacy; Encouraging the Heart; The Student Leadership Challenge;* and *The Academic Administrator's Guide to Exemplary Leadership.* They also developed the highly acclaimed Leadership Practices Inventory (LPI), a 360-degree questionnaire for assessing leadership behavior that is one of the most widely used leadership assessment instruments in the world, along with The Student LPI. The Five Practices of Exemplary Leadership model they developed has been the basis of more than six hundred doctoral dissertations and academic research projects (a summary of these is available at www.theleadershipchallenge .com/research).

Among the honors and awards that Jim and Barry have received is the American Society for Training and Development's highest award for their Distinguished Contribution to Workplace Learning and Performance. They have been named Management/Leadership Educators of the Year by the International Management Council; ranked by *Leadership Excellence* magazine in the top twenty on its list of the Top 100 Thought Leaders; named among the Top 50 Leadership Coaches in the nation (according to *Coaching for Leadership*); and listed among *HR Magazine*'s Most Influential Thinkers in the World.

Jim and Barry are frequent speakers, and each has conducted leadership development programs for organizations such as Apple, Applied Materials, ARCO, AT&T, Australia Institute of Management, Australia Post, Bank of America, Bose, Charles Schwab, Cisco Systems, Clorox, Community Leadership Association, Conference Board of Canada, Consumers Energy, Deloitte Touche, Dorothy Wylie Nursing Leadership Institute, Dow Chemical, Egon Zehnder International, Federal Express, Genentech, Google, Gymboree, HP, IBM, Jobs DR-Singapore, Johnson & Johnson, Kaiser Foundation Health Plans and Hospitals, Intel, Itau Unibanco, L.L. Bean, Lawrence Livermore National Labs, Lucile Packard Children's Hospital, Merck, Motorola, NetApp, Northrop Grumman, Novartis, Nvidia, Oakwood Housing, Oracle, Petronas, Roche Bioscience, Siemens, 3M, Toyota, United Way, USAA, Verizon, VISA, the Walt Disney Company, and Westpac. They have lectured at over sixty college and university campuses around the globe.

More information about Jim and Barry and their work, research, and services can be found at www.theleadershipchallenge.com.

• • •

James M. Kouzes is the Dean's Executive Fellow of Leadership, Leavey School of Business, at Santa Clara University, and lectures on leadership around the world to corporations, governments, and nonprofits. He is a highly regarded leadership scholar and an experienced executive; the *Wall Street Journal* has cited him as one of the twelve best executive educators in the United States. In 2010, Jim received the Thought Leadership Award from the Instructional Systems Association, the most prestigious award given by the trade association of training and development industry providers. In 2006, he received the Golden Gavel, the highest honor awarded by Toastmasters International.

Jim served as president, CEO, and chairman of The Tom Peters Company from 1988 through 1999 and prior to that led the Executive Development Center at Santa Clara University (1981–1987). He founded the Joint Center for Human Services Development at San Jose State University (1972–1980) and was on the staff of the School of Social Work, University of Texas. His career in training and development began in 1969 when he conducted seminars for Community Action Agency staff and volunteers in the war on poverty. Following graduation from Michigan State University (BA with honors in political science), he served as a Peace Corps volunteer (1967–1969). Jim can be reached at jim@kouzes.com.

• • •

Barry Z. Posner is the Michael J. Accolti, S.J., Endowed Professor of Leadership at the Leavey School of Business, Santa Clara University, where he served as dean of the school for twelve years (1997–2009). He has been a distinguished visiting professor at Hong Kong University of Science and Technology, Sabanci University (Istanbul), and the University of Western Australia. At Santa Clara, he has received the President's Distinguished Faculty Award, the school's Extraordinary Faculty Award, and several other teaching and academic honors. An internationally renowned scholar and educator, Barry is the author or coauthor of more than one hundred research and practitioner-focused articles. He currently serves on the editorial advisory boards for *Leadership and Organizational Development Journal* and the *International Journal of Servant-Leadership*. In 2011, he received the Outstanding Scholar Award from the *Journal of Management Inquiry.*

Barry received his BA (with honors) in political science from the University of California, Santa Barbara; his MA in public administration from The Ohio State University; and his PhD in organizational behavior and administrative theory from the University of Massachusetts. Having consulted with a wide variety of public and private sector organizations around the globe, Barry also works at a strategic level with a number of community-based and professional organizations, currently sitting on the board of directors of EMQ FamiliesFirst and the Global Women's Leadership Network. He has served previously on the boards of the American Institute of Architects, Big Brothers/Big Sisters of Santa Clara County, Center for Excellence in Nonprofits, Junior Achievement of Silicon Valley and Monterey Bay, Public Allies, San Jose Repertory Theater, Sigma Phi Epsilon Fraternity, and several start-up companies. Barry can be reached at bposner@scu.edu.

• • •

Beth High is an author, organizational consultant, program designer, coach, keynote speaker, and Certified Master Facilitator. Her work in these areas has allowed her to develop a strong client list from a variety of sectors, including Capital One; Girls, Inc.; John Wiley and Sons, England and Dubai; KalTire Canada; North Carolina Department of Transportation; SAS and SAS Asia Pacific; Saudi Arabia Ministry of Education; Western Union; University of Arkansas; University of North Carolina School of Government; University of North Carolina School of Business; and VF Jeanswear. She is president of High Road Consulting, a leadership development company based in Chapel Hill, North Carolina.

She has produced the Leadercast Series, a podcast series with authors Jim Kouzes and Barry Posner, and developed a Jossey-Bass Certification Program for educators interested in developing programs based on The Student Leadership Challenge. The unique blended learning approach for this program allowed Beth to create the platform on which The Leadership Challenge Workshop Online® was subsequently created. This work resulted in the creation of her partner company, HRCPartners, which focuses solely on the development and implementation of The Leadership Challenge Workshop Online and the FollowThruOnline product platforms.

Beth regularly delivers The Leadership Challenge® Workshop in a variety of formats and consults with companies globally on how to incorporate The Five Practices model into their existing leadership programs. Having completed an M.ED. in instructional design and educational media at the University of North Carolina, Chapel Hill, she is committed to top quality design of programs that explore new technologies while addressing the unique learning and development needs of the audience. Her expertise enables her to consult, design, and deliver long-format programs, lasting from eighteen to twenty-four months, built around virtual centers and using a blended learning approach. Beth and her team work closely with clients to customize program content and capture the appropriate data these sites provide. These centers allow participants to have the extended practice essential for building skills and provide the program owners with evidence of return on investment from the training. Beth can be reached at highroadconsulting@gmail.com.

• • •

Gary M. Morgan has taught or developed student leadership courses and programs at universities of all sizes for the past twenty years. He has served as a dean, director, and faculty member at campuses with enrollments ranging from twelve hundred to fifty-three thousand students and directed programs or services in student leadership, student activities and programming, student government, Greek life, residence life, orientation, the student union, judicial affairs, graduate schools and graduate student life, volunteer and community services, and many other areas. He has always held positions that had a focus on developing students as leaders. In addition to his college-level work, he has developed leadership education programs for high school students in Upward Bound and recently created a summer-long leadership program for foster youth for an Orlando, Florida, community organization.

Gary received a bachelor of science degree in communication studies (radio/TV/film) from Northern Illinois University and a master of arts degree in higher education–college student personnel from Bowling Green State University. He completed the doctoral course work and exam requirements for the Ph.D. in higher education administration at the University of South Carolina. He is a certified facilitator for The Leadership Challenge™ and Student Leadership Challenge™ and is the founder and CEO of the Student Leadership Excellence Academy and the Leadership Excellence Academy. He is a member of the American College Personnel Association, Student Affairs Administrators in Higher Education, American Society for Training and Development, International Leadership Association, and the National Clearinghouse for Leadership Programs. Gary can be contacted at gary@student-leader.com.